TEIGNMOUTH AND IT'S PEOPLE

1935 to 1953

Written & Published by Viv Wilson MBE

First Published October 2005
© Viv Wilson 2005

Designed and Printed by
Exe Print, Exeter

ISBN: 0-9539523-3-9

SINCERE THANKS TO

The many people of Teignmouth who contributed
photographs and memories
Alice Cross Centre
Teignmouth & Shaldon Museum
Exe Print, Exeter
Proof readers - Pauline Rossi and Jim Stowers QPM

BIBLIOGRAPHY

The years shown refer to initial publication dates
History of Teignmouth – Grace Griffiths 1973
Teignmouth – HJ Trump 1976
Teignmouth Post Newspapers
Teignmouth at War Book 1 – Viv Wilson 2000
Teignmouth at War Book 2 – Viv Wilson 2002
Dorothy of Hythe in Kent – Ruth I Johns www.plowrightpress.co.uk
Yours Sincerely Morgan Giles – Virginia Jane Northcote 1995
Teignmouth's Haldon Aerodrome – Keith A Saunders 1999

DISCLAIMER

All information, other than newspaper articles, included in this book
has been recorded in good faith by the author who offers it as collected
memories from those who lived through this period

DEDICATION

This book is dedicated to the 28th Construction Battalion, US Navy

The Seabees, who "invaded" Teignmouth in 1944, made many friends and created life-long memories. Links were re-forged via email in 2004, resulting in the gift of a set of original photographs taken by The Seabees during their time here. These unique images, reproduced to the largest format in Chapter 4, are the centrepiece of this book.

Bruno Petruccione and the plaque of 1944

Bruno Petruccione, former Master at Arms is pictured at a reunion of the 28th Battalion Construction Battalion of the US Navy. The plaque is one of only five made in 1944. When The Seabees were based at Teignmouth during that year, the Den Pavilion became their mess hall.

Bruno sent the plaque to me in 2005 with a message that it was time for it to find a resting place and it was fitting that it should be their old mess hall.

"We know that it will be secure and receive the treatment that we feel it deserves. To the people of Teignmouth, our belated thanks for their hospitality and our admiration for their "conduct under fire" during the war.

AUTHOR'S INTRODUCTION

Sometime in 2002, Teignmouth Players faced the possibility of termination of their lease on the Carlton Theatre. At a meeting to discuss other options, I became preoccupied with thoughts of my own relationship with the theatre, now over 70 years old. My first visit was to watch my aunt on stage with Teignmouth Operatic Society in 1958. I followed in her footsteps and for a quarter of a century, had the joy of participating in plays, shows and pantomimes as well as presenting slide shows there.

I was aware that US troops had used the building during the war and understood that some of them lost their lives at Slapton. I wondered if, by dedicating the site as American soil for all time, as has happened elsewhere, the future of the building could be protected. I put the idea to John Branch, Players Chairman, hoping it might lead to an opportunity to embrace the past in a positive way. It could help quash negative aspects about the building that had been voiced for years. Player, Roger Smith decided to search for details of the battalion through the Internet and approached a contact who works in the Pentagon. The search proved fruitful. Roger located Bruno Petruccione of the US Navy 28th Construction Battalion that took Teignmouth by storm in 1944.

The idea of involving the USA to save the theatre was, perhaps, a little far-fetched but the benefit of making contact with Bruno is the book that you are now holding. After a year or two of email contact, Bruno generously rounded up a batch of photographs that simply had to be shared. Reproduced to the largest possible format, they provide a detailed insight of an extraordinary period in Teignmouth's past. Bruno planned to return to Teignmouth with his wife in June 2005 for the 60th Anniversary of VE&VJ Days. He was to bring a magnificent wooden plaque made by the Seabees in 1944 to put on permanent display in the Carlton Theatre, their wartime mess hall. Early in January, he sustained severe injuries to his arm in a road accident. Unable to make the trip, he posted the plaque and I had the honour to present it publicly to Teignmouth's Mayor, Cllr Geoff Bladon on 19th June 2005. Beryl King as Curator, accepted permanent ownership on behalf of Teignmouth & Shaldon Museum. Roger Smith of the Teignmouth Players received the plaque and arranged for this unique piece of history to be displayed permanently in the foyer of the Carlton Theatre. The public unveiling took place on 21st August 2005.

Having been born nine months after VE Day, I consider myself to be a Victory Baby. Adults frequently referred to events as being "before the war" when I was growing up. Fears for world peace in the 1960s placed the subject of war beyond discussion in my personal sphere, a state that lasted for 20 years.

Involvement in Teignmouth's history made the topic unavoidable. After publishing Teignmouth at War Books 1 and 2 and generating enormous interest, it had been my intention to draw a firm line. The era on either side of the conflict and roughly enclosed by two coronations was the obvious solution.

Some people claim they cannot remember much when approached for material. The truth is that even tiny memories sewn together help extend the picture. These shreds often answer a question or put another fact into perspective. Even momentary emotions deserve to be recorded since they are another splash of colour on the never-ending canvas of human memory.

Viv Wilson MBE

Teignmouth 2005

FOREWORD by Cllr MARY STRUDWICK
Alderman of Devon and Mayor of Teignmouth 2004-5

The day war was declared on Germany, Sunday, 3rd September 1939, I was 7 years old and my sister Jenny, five years younger. We were staying with our grandmother in Essex. The next day my father hired a car and drove us back to our home in London beneath a sky full of sinister-looking grey fish-like objects that were going to keep us safe from German aircraft. The following day, we were driven to Devon to live with my father's mother and sister. We did not know them and I remember feeling totally abandoned when my parents left. We had each other, our teddy bears and our gas masks. Mine was black and smelly and Jenny's was Mickey Mouse shaped. Life at Clapperland Lodge, situated at the gates of the Clifford Estate of Ugbrooke, was very different from London. The thatched cottage, set in a large garden, had no gas or electricity, only a cold water tap in the kitchen and a lavatory outside the back door. The nearest neighbour was half a mile away. The school, with it's nine pupils, was a two-mile walk through the estate to Biddlecombe. In the summer of 1940, Father Biggs, the Catholic Priest organized a school outing to the convent at Teignmouth. After lunch we were taken down to the seafront. I clearly remember the excitement of approaching the seaside followed by the shock of finding rolls of barbed wire stretched along the front. It was the first of many visits and the beginning of my love of the town over the following 60 years. I later worked with Grace Griffiths, the local historian when Teignmouth Library was on Fore Street. We never returned to London and had the privilege of being nurtured and educated in Devon, like our father. I pray that our families will never again be separated and frightened as so many of us were.

In collecting and recording these memories, Viv Wilson has created a fascinating archive. Together with her books on the history of Teignmouth, historians will be indebted to her, future researchers will find a valuable resource and it will start a chain of memories for many of her readers. I am grateful to her for allowing me to join in with this experience.

Mary Strudwick nee Candish (R) and sister Jenny, 1940
Evacuated to their grandmother's home on Lord Clifford's Estate at Ugbrooke, Chudleigh

CHAPTER 1

Into each life some rain must fall

The hungry '30s...families survive on very little...
the inevitability of another war with Germany... .....The Great Deluge.

Many Teignmouth people remember the1930s when work and food were in short supply. Children were sent to bakery shops to buy yesterday's bread and the Soup Kitchen in Willey Lane kept many families going through the winters. Career prospects amounted to very little, the boys were involved in fishing and most of them belonged to the Royal Navy Reserve. The girls were joined by an influx of females from Wales seeking a position "in service". A veritable army of young women executed the domestic requirements in numerous large residences on the hillsides. The town was awash with shops and services employing larger numbers of staff than would be expected now, who worked for little reward. People were very resourceful in making ends meet and their expectations from life were modest. The coming war would broaden their limited horizons. Those who lived through the era claim that despite deprivations, life was enjoyable and people cared more for one another.

The Riviera, 1937
Upgraded to the latest super-cinema style in 1934, it advertises showings of the Grand Coronation Procession, recorded when King George VI and his Queen were crowned in 1937.

Fishing near the Point
Local fishermen haul in a gigantic catch. A large net and a small boat helped keep families afloat during the lean times.

TUDC workhorse at Gales Hill
Bedecked with the traditional regalia for a show, the horse stands in the council yard next to Sun Lane. Horsepower was about to be overtaken by motor vehicles.

Parson Place

Peggy Hatherly in The Court that stood at right angles to Parson St. The tiny cottages were swept away by post-war development. The building in the background was the Regia Hotel, converted to flats in the 1990s.

Promenade Photo Shop

Before cameras were commonplace, a council-licensed photographer captured images of promenade strollers and processed the films in the hut. When war came, the contents were tipped on the beach, locals raking through to save photos of themselves and their friends.

Carnival float on the seafront

The battleship carnival float, built over a lorry with the registration DV 9553, was topical. Mr James, (third from left) a former Chairman of Teignmouth Urban District Council has sportingly dressed up as a sailor.

Carnival float at Lower Bitton

Bert Russell and Albert Taylor, two notable fun merchants, portray Queen and King in 1937, Coronation Year. Two beautiful attendants and a diminutive guardsman adorn the float. The Cricket Club used the redundant railway carriage as changing rooms.

Display of Patriotism
Britannia's Silent Toast expresses the hope for peace in the 1937 Carnival. The queen receives her crown, acknowledging the Coronation of King George VI and Queen Elizabeth. Three children wear the national costumes of Ireland, Scotland and Wales. Neta Drew stands by the star, right.

Darke's Milk Bar
The first of its kind in the area, the window provides a glimpse of Lee's Tofferie across Regent Street.

Golden Hind replica, 1938
Pixie Matthews (L) and his son Bill near the Fishermen's Lamp at the Point. Teignmouth Urban District Council commissioned Pixie to build the replica for the opening of the new promenade yachting pool.

Pride of the Teign
Bill Bulley built this boat. Ivy Ware stands left and her mother Alice is seated, second right. SH Ware, a specialist tea and coffee importer, had a retail shop in Northumberland Place. Flat-roofed houses, newly built at Inverteign Drive are in the distance, to the right of the bridge.

Bank Street

A plane was usually displayed in the windows of WR Parkhouse's Agra Auto and Aero Engineering shop premises, but it is not visible in this photograph. FW Woolworth took over the store.

Flying lessons

After developing Haldon Aerodrome in 1929, WR Parkhouse trained several pilots. With war on the horizon, Britain needed good pilots on standby. Duggie Gourd, renowned local coach driver, is pictured climbing into a light aircraft for a lesson at Haldon.

Red Cross at the Aerodrome

Air circuses drew huge crowds and the Red Cross attended such major events. Edward, Prince of Wales, stopped off at Haldon Aerodrome during a visit to the westcountry in 1931.

Rhonsperber glider

Barbara Jenkins, a teacher at Lendrick School, took this photograph at Haldon Aerodrome in 1937. One might speculate that she considered the presence of a German craft significant at this time.

From Lendrick School windows

Another photograph taken by Barbara Jenkins. Beyond the tennis courts and putting green, a whalebone arch is visible to the left of the promenade shelter.

Teignmouth Territorial Army Band

Formed by Bill Hooper in the 1930s, the local musicians are on the right of the picture. Taken at Bulford Camp, Wiltshire in 1938, members' names include Ripley, Jones, Banham, Corbyn, Davey, Mott, Mole, McGinn and Winstanley.

In 1939, the Band and Teignmouth TA went to Chickerell Camp, Weymouth as the 5th Battalion Prince of Wales Devon's TA. They returned as the 7th Battalion Haytor Devon's TA.

In 1941, the regiment became the 87th Anti Tank Regiment, Royal Artillery. They moved back to Chagford then on to North Africa. The regimental band gained an excellent reputation in the Middle East Command and was kept going until the end of the war, even though the regiment itself was disbanded in May 1944.

Esplanade Hotel

The Esplanade Hotel was one of many large seafront establishments that could collectively provide accommodation for about 2000 visitors at a time. Most large buildings in town were soon to be requisitioned for troops' billets. Esplanade Hotel was destroyed in September 1942.

River Beach, 1938

The peaceful nature of this stretch would soon be disrupted and block walls built across the adjoining lanes to combat the threat of invasion. Within two years, the Admiralty would begin requisitioning small boats after acquiring use of the harbour in exchange for £200. The Lifeboat Station would close and half a century pass before it reopened

Pike Ward's whalebone arch

Installed at the far end of Old Maids' Walk early in the 20th century, it was removed to make way for the emplacement of a large gun early in the war.

Town Hall, Brunswick Street

The upper floor, resplendent with snowy white tablecloths and floral decorations, is prepared for a function. It would not be long before this space would be used to train people to deal with gas attacks and air strikes. The building was destroyed by enemy action on 13th August 1942. The remaining portion, once the Library, currently serves as a public toilet.

His Majesty King George VI Coronation.

Teignmouth Celebrations.

CHILDREN'S TEA.

TOWN HALL BUILDINGS.
MAY 12TH 1937, 5 P.M.

Please admit Pat Brown

GOD SAVE THE KING.

NOT TRANSFERABLE.

Nº 211

Invitation to Teignmouth Celebrations

At 09.50 on 12th May 1937, pupils processed from Brook Hill School yard to the Den for a service to mark King George VI and Queen Elizabeth's Coronation. Pat Penwill nee Brown remembers the celebratory children's tea in the upper floor of the Town Hall. The tables were laid out in long rows and tea included "Tuff" cakes - a bread roll, split and spread with jam and a daub of cream. Webber the Baker sold these at a farthing each. A Coronation mug and hardback book about King George VI was given to each child. High temperatures caused people to faint yet the following day brought a freak fall of snow.

The Great Deluge, 21st July 1939

Teignmouth experienced a " Deluge of Biblical Proportions". Charlie Smale the window cleaner stands with his cart outside Richards Boot and Shoe Repair shop at 24 Brunswick Street, since renumbered to 28. The Town Hall is on the right.

Den Road & Waterloo Street

Storms, wind, high tide and an inefficient drainage system caused widespread flooding. The Belisha beacon marks the Den Road crossing.

Dawlish Street

Sea defences were weak at the east end of town until major work was completed early in the 1990s. Tudor House Private Hotel stood next to the Undertaker, Brook Bullen & Company.

Station Road

Teignmouth's annual carnival banner hangs across the road and a large group of people has gathered at the top, outside the gates to station yard to see the extent of the flooding.

The Triangle
A coach is parked by Teign Cars booking office in Lower Brook Street as the crowds stand beside the floodwater, witnessing an unforgettable day.

Bank Street
International Stores and other retailers suffered loss of stock in the cellars. Even now, the lower ground floors experience flooding at times.

TUDC Steam Roller

Stan Apps was the foreman when these improvements were made to the road surface in front of Courtenay Terrace in the 1930s. The number of motorcars was beginning to increase significantly.

The Swan

This exquisite float pictured outside Courtenay House appeared in several carnivals during this decade.

Bill Rose at Hoare's Taxi Office in Station Road

One-time driver of a horse-drawn carriage, Bill moved with the times and drove taxis. Given a task of 'National Importance' in wartime, he moved his family to Abingdon and became a driver of Queen Mary low-loaders that transported aircraft and their engines.

St Michaels' Brownie Pack c.1935

The girls often fried supper on this plot in Barnpark Road.

Back row L-R: Doreen Penwill, Beryl Cook, Pauline Rose, Peggy Gillard, Martin the dog owned by Brown Owl, Anne Wright.

Front row L-R: Iris Street, Joan Mills, Beryl Woolway.

382 Battery Territorial Army, Royal Devon Yeomanry, 96th Field Regiment. R.A. Salisbury Plain camp July 1939
Back row L-R: L Bennett, D Brown, S Causley, and W Steer
Front row L-R: W Tidball, V Studd, and G Wise
Stan Causley was one of many local lads in the Devonshire Regiment TA who trained in the Drill Hall next to Brook Hill School. Other Teignmothian friends in the Yeomanry were Ern and Bill Shimmell, Eddie Hobart, Peter Pierce, Harold Rodwell, Fred Medland and The Nathans - Noel, Basil, Roy and Cecil.

Brook Hill School Teachers
Back row L-R: Student teacher, Miss Stanbury, and Miss Hilda Best
Front row L-R: Sallie Such, Miss Hayman and Miss Wardle

Chapter 2

War comes but life goes on

Arrival of evacuees.......living with anxiety......
putting on a brave face and trying to make the best of things.

At the declaration of war, 44 million respirators had already been distributed throughout the country in anticipation of poison gas attacks. Children under 2 years were protected by baby bags, resembling a knapsack with a Perspex visor, which had to have air pumped into them. Mickey Mouse-shaped respirators with blue rings round the eyes and red rubber trimmings were given to children aged 2 to 5. Large rattles, such as those seen at football matches were issued to Air Raid Precaution wardens to whirl when an air strike occurred, but they were never used. In Operation Pied Piper, 1.9 million children were evacuated from cities thought likely to be targeted.

Teignmouth people felt the war was far away until the Battle of Britain took place in June 1940. One month later, enemy planes dropped two bombs beside the pier during the first of 22 air raids.

Don't you know there's a war on?
Twins, Fred & Gladys Laurie and a friend (R) on east beach. The barricade of scaffold poles did not deter fun or sun-seeking on the sands.

Teignmouth promenade

Audrey Sharp nee Richards and husband Joe, on Embarkation Leave from the RAF 11th July 1941. Joe was reported missing from Singapore a year later. A telegram arrived after several weeks, "Safe and well in Australia after several hours in the sea off the coast of Singapore - Joe."

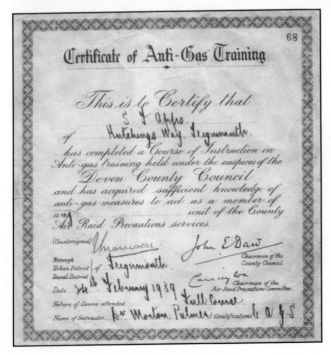

Certificate of Anti-Gas Training

Devon County Council organized training to prepare people to deal with gas attacks. Brigadier Morrison, Teignmouth's Chief ARP warden signed Stan Apps' certificate seven months before the start of hostilities.

Two evacuees join a local family
Stan Apps' mother, Kate at her Bitton Terrace home with grandchildren, Ann on her lap, Mary (left) and John behind. The girl and boy on the right are evacuees, Eileen and John Waters.

Donald H Robinson

At the outbreak of war I was aged 4. I recall being driven over Haldon in the family car and seeing what looked like sawn-off telegraph poles or pit props stuck in the ground all over the moor, airfield and golf course to stop enemy planes from landing. Also, my father, J.Hedley Robinson sometimes went missing during the night. It turned out that he was involved with something called Civil Defence. He and half a dozen men spent the nights in a hut on Haldon, each armed with a stout stick with a lump of lead on top of it, in case a German Panzer Division (500+ heavily armed men all fully trained) parachuted down. If things got really serious, they had a telephone to call for military armoured back-up in the form of a dilapidated truck based at Chudleigh! Experiments with aerial mines also took place up there. The project involved suspending explosives from tethered balloons, rigged to explode on detecting the approach of an aircraft. It was abandoned, possibly due to the difficulty in telling the difference between the engine of a Heinkel 111 and an Avro Lancaster!

In Dad's ARP helmet, 1941

Dad was turned down on medical grounds when he volunteered for the Navy. He kept on his job at Midland Bank and worked as an Intelligence Officer with Brigadier Morrison at the ARP HQ in the cellars of Bitton House. We lived in Inverteign Drive in a pair of semi-detached bungalows next to my maternal grandparents, Hodgson and Rebecca Fletcher. Grandfather dug out the earth under the front dining room to make an air raid shelter for us all with a trap door for access and an escape passage. The war seemed a long way off until the evening of Sunday 7th July 1940 when Mum and I were walking along the seafront. I asked if we could go on the pier but Mum, being a strict Methodist refused because it was Sunday. Like most kids, I kept on and she finally relented and we went out as far as the turnstile at the end of the middle section then turned back. Suddenly, the roar of aircraft engines interrupted the peaceful atmosphere and a Junkers 88 came at us from the direction of the Ness. It flew over the pier and dropped a bomb on either side. It was so quick that we hardly saw the plane but heard the explosions and screams. A soldier had thrown us to the ground and sheltered us from flying glass splinters and shards with his own body. Once the panic had stopped, he hoisted me on his shoulder and escorted us to the Riviera Cinema where Dad had arranged to pick us up. Dad had seen the whole thing through his binoculars from home. Knowing that we were in the area one can only imagine his feelings. Mum considered the episode to be "Divine Retribution" of some kind and never ventured on the pier on a Sunday again!

Milhedon Bungalow in Inverteign Drive with estuary views
Albert, the first evacuee to stay with the Robinson family and 5-year old Donald on his bike.

On the beach at Shaldon
Donald with Helen Edna Moss, evacuated with the family from September 1940 to May 1941.

At 2.15am on 8th May 1941, we woke to the terrifying sound of bombs exploding on the hospital only 200 yards away. We were under the floor in our shelter and everything was shaking as if it was an earthquake. I shall never forget the explosions, vibrations, the sound of falling debris, the feeling of total helplessness and claustrophobia; it seemed to go on forever. We had a little Jewish evacuee called Helen Moss staying with us and it must have been worse for her – at least I had my family with me except that Dad was on duty. In the morning, we found a brick gatepost embedded upright in the middle of our front lawn but never discovered from whence it came. Helen and I were sent to school as usual and as we walked hand in hand down Inverteign, we found it impossible to set foot on the ground without walking on roof tiles blown off during the raid. On his way home, Dad passed the hospital and discovered the rescue workers were unable to reach people trapped beneath a very large piece of flooring pinned down by fallen rubble. He raced along the back lane to fetch my grandfather, Hodgson Fletcher, who was a retired builder. He brought his handsaw and cut through 15 to 20 feet of stout floorboards non-stop at breakneck speed. This amazed everyone – not bad for a man of 63! The casualties were then released. Another casualty of that raid was a lovely wooden railway engine, big enough for me to sit astride and trundle round on. Dad had made it for me and it was stored in the washhouse but a piece of masonry crashed through the roof and smashed it to bits. It was at this point that a certain 5-year-old boy decided that the enemy was definitely not nice!

The final straw came when my grandfather got out of his armchair for no particular reason and went to the other side of the room and a hundredweight or so of masonry smashed through the roof and ceiling and fell on to his armchair. By that time I was very jumpy and nervous and was frightened every time I saw or heard an aircraft. I wouldn't play in the back garden unless the door was left open for me to run indoors if there was a plane around. It was agreed that we should all move to stay with a Methodist Minister and his wife at Whiddon Down. Because of his job and ARP commitments, Dad stayed on and found lodgings with Miss Jocelyn at the Anchorage, Yannon Drive. Helen went to another family in Teignmouth and I heard later that when she returned there after an air raid, only the doorstep of the house was still standing. Jewish children mustered in the Baptist Hall for schooling and emergencies.

Hodgson Fletcher
Donald's grandfather released people trapped beneath rubble after Teignmouth Hospital was bombed.

Dad's experiences were classified and he was very conscientious but in later years, he felt it was all right to tell me a little of what went on. One of the problems with the "hit and run" raids was that the average warning was no longer than 90 seconds. The attackers came in low over the sea, often unseen, machine-gunning the town on their approach. They dropped their first lot of bombs, flew up the estuary, turned back downriver with guns blazing and dropping remaining bombs before streaking out to sea. The sirens usually sounded afterwards. Several attempts were made to improve the speed of the alarm system. A permanent lookout was positioned on top of the headland by Parson & Clerk Rocks. He had binoculars and a button to sound the alarm direct but it did not work. The RAF put a patrol of Hurricanes 5 miles out at sea 24 hours a day but the enemy still got through. The distinctive Teign estuary, running east west, was a useful landmark to bomber pilots at high altitude on a dark night. At the meeting of fresh and salt water, a faint luminescence occurs that could be clearly seen from high up. The raiders simply had to find the shining river, take their bearings from it to reach their target.

Mary Tapper, my late mother-in-law lived above the family's furniture shop at Orchard Gardens. When her eldest daughter Joan returned home from Brook Hill School following a raid, she was covered in plaster dust from a collapsed ceiling. Her little sister Valerie had been playing near the fireplace when vibrations from the bomb loosened chimney soot. Poor Mary had to clean up two little girls - one completely black and the other completely white!

Rocket guns were installed that could fire 2 to 25 missiles simultaneously or singly, usually the former and made an unbelievable noise. We returned to Teignmouth in late 1944 and I recall the multitude of bombsites on which we played. The most vivid memories of VE Day, apart from the flags decorating the town, were watching the remaining troops having a giant bonfire in the middle of the road outside the Courtenay Hotel. Wardrobes, chairs, beds and tables were pushed out of the windows and thrown on the fire and nobody seemed to mind! I've never experienced such an atmosphere! Let's not lay all the blame on British lads as quite a few Yanks lent a hand too. It was a case of Anglo-American co-operation to the very end!

Webber the Baker
The rounds man, delivering to Inverteign Drive, makes sure Donald and his friend do not see the goods inside the van.

J Hedley Robinson
Hedley was Teignmouth's ARP Intelligence Officer based at Bitton House. After the war, he built two astronomical observatories in his garden at Inverteign Drive. One of them, together with his telescope were donated to Teignmouth Grammar School.

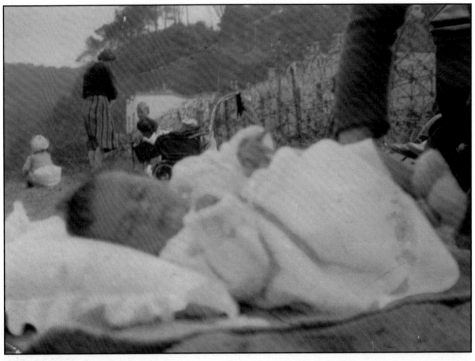

Summer of 1940, Shaldon
A barbed wire barrier constructed along the beach helped protect Shaldon
from invasion. Baby James Lakeman and children further along are blissfully
unaware of the impending danger.

Ray Rann

Ray was only 4 years old when his parents drove him from Hackney to
Teignmouth. Too young to be an evacuee, his father had seen an
advertisement for a small preparatory school with boarding at Stapleford.
Situated on the south side of New Road, the school was run by a Mrs Howard
whose husband was a veteran of World War One. Their four sons and
daughter were away serving their country. She believed in intense education
and strict discipline for the 20 boys and girls. The pupils were once strafed
with machine gun bullets in the garden. They walked in crocodile fashion
each Sunday for the service at St James Church. Ray remembers its lovely
ceiling with the golden moon and stars. They were allowed to visit the beach
and he can still relive the sensation of climbing through and somersaulting on
the anti-invasion barrier. The rust got into his eyes - and sandwiches! After
being forced out of Stapleford, they moved to another building across the

road then on to Avonwick where they were allowed to occupy half the manor house belonging to Squire Cornish Bowden. Ray learned to love the land through its home farm and helped with haymaking and potato gathering. They met some US servicemen based at nearby Slapton who taught them knife-throwing at trees and other tricks. Ray went into the world of advertising and printing in Knightsbridge, and has retired to a farm near Bude but remembers Teignmouth with great affection.

Stapleford House, early 20th century
It was a private boarding school for young children, displaced by war.

Joy Puttock nee Wills

As a small child I had one or two wonderful summer holidays in Teignmouth with my parents in Exeter Street. In 1939 I was evacuated from London with Haberdasher Aske's school to Hove. Sharing with Hove School did not work out and a week before Christmas we were told that we were moving on to an unknown destination. We boarded the train with a little luggage, evacuee labels and gas masks. The train eventually stopped at Teignmouth and I was so thrilled! We were taken to the Den Pavilion and from there, a few at a time, we went off to our new "homes". I was one of six taken to a hotel in Powderham Terrace run by Mr & Mrs Councer. I believe it was this place that received a direct hit in January 1943. There were no air raids at this time and the owners were hoping for holidaymakers so in the spring they wanted us out. We were split up, four of us went to an old lady who lived near the

Golden Lion and conditions were not good. Food was scant and the house was very damp. After two weeks we moved in with Mrs Brock at Luny Cottage and this time all was well - very well!

We joined with the choir of St James Church, rehearsing for Stainer's Crucifixion in the weeks leading up to Easter 1940. Even now, when that music is played, I am immediately transported back to Teignmouth. We shared with Teignmouth Grammar School and, as far as I am aware, all went smoothly. I was so proud of my hockey stick stained red with Devon soil!

In the June we sat Matriculation Exams and during the Latin paper, a German plane jettisoned a bomb near the pier. We spent most of the exam time under the desk and that was fine by me because I couldn't do it and wrote an account of events on the back of the exam paper instead!

I returned home to Plumstead intending to return to Teignmouth at the start of the autumn term but it was not to be. I trained at Brighton Training College for Teachers, returning to Teignmouth for a week's holiday with Mrs Brock. We all went to a Teign Street pub to celebrate VJ day. We have made many family visits to the town ever since and I find it hard to leave.

In the garden at Luny Cottage, Teign Street, 1940
Joy Wills (right) aged 16 and 3 friends, Connie Thorpe, Dorothy Cutler and Pat McGrath, known as The Four Musketeers, evacuees from Haberdasher Aske's School.

Shirley Ingram nee Collins

I was a pupil of Teignmouth Preparatory School from 1940-46. Mr Sidney Silverston was the Principal and also Headmaster of the Grammar School. Lessons took place in a large wooden hut near the bottom of the Grammar School playing fields. There were between 20 and 30 pupils and our teachers were Miss Lynn, Miss Seal and Miss Everson. We had to have school dinners because of the bombing raids. The cabbage was awful but the jam tart and custard were lovely! It was a very happy atmosphere and I thoroughly enjoyed my time there.

Teignmouth Preparatory School pupils in the Grammar School grounds, 1943

Back row L-R: John Hayman, Pauline Lloyd Williams, Wendy Avery, Noel Armstead, Jean Northcott, Rachel Vaughn Williams, Shirley Silverston, David Stent, Laurence Sercombe, Eric Robjohns,

Front row L-R: Anne Williams, Valerie Blackmore, Christine Bullock, Anne Symons, and Ann Hirons

Teignmouth Gas Works
Bombs were dropped on the railway line and the hills close to Headway Cross, above Broadmeadow. The following three memories relate to this area.

Keith Sanders

Whilst clearing my mother's home in 2004, I found a postcard dated 9th September 1943 posted in Newton Abbot and telling my grandfather that we were coming home early. We had planned to spend a fortnight with relatives in Kingsteignton. Memories of a head-on attack by a JU88 on the train came flooding back. The sight of a very angry plane with red stabs of flame from what I now know to be six 20mm cannon, dancing around the nose has remained with me ever since.

A Bishopsteignton Girl

When a stick of bombs was emptied on Coombe Way, just beyond Teignmouth's boundary, some village children went up to look at the craters. One was in the hedge below Headway Cross and two more in the fields immediately to the east, close to where Inverteign School now stands. It was the first time she had seen a black American and he warned her to stay away from the craters for her own safety. Growing up in Bishopsteignton in wartime was adventuresome and she was lucky to escape unscathed when an enemy plane laced the river with machine gun bullets whilst she was having a swim.

News that a field was being harvested sent village children scurrying off, a bottle of water and jam sandwich in their pocket. They carried a stout stick to despatch any rabbits that broke cover during harvest. They had no qualms about this since a rabbit made a meal for the family in those hungry times.

Tom Radford

Bombs fell in fields near Headway Cross where Tom and his pals met the Bishopsteignton boys to roam free and stage boxing competitions. Halfway down the road down to Coombe from Headway, a large indent in the hedge still marks the spot where one of the bombs fell. It hit the water main that carried the supply from Paignton to Teignmouth reservoir and water spouted to a great height.

*See the photograph of the bomb crater in Chapter 6.

Eileen Aggett

Eileen Aggett nee Kelly worked as a cook general for Mr Proctor the Solicitor at Algoa Lodge at Coombe Road and later, for Dr Burbury at White Lodge. In 1940, she married Bob Aggett, a mechanic at Broadbear's Garage, Regent Street and they moved in with Bob's parents at 15 Coombe Vale Rd. Bob began his war service with RAOC then graduated to REME, repairing cars and tanks. During the Africa campaign, the soldiers did not have the luxury of Red Cross parcels. Two Salvation Army ladies of mature years attached themselves to the regiment, darning socks and cooking rock buns for the soldiers during their advance through the desert. At home in Teignmouth, Bob's father, a representative for Brittanic Insurance served the community as an air raid warden patrolling the area of Coombe. He saved the lives of Eileen and his wife when an enemy plane strafed the seafront with bullets by throwing them under the seat in a shelter and shielding them with his body. The sound of shattering glass was all around them and they thought their end had come. After the installation of a Morrison shelter and the birth of baby Mary in 1941, the house was too cramped so Eileen moved into Cosy Nook, a one-down, one-up cottage with a rear scullery, further along the road. Her second daughter, Betty arrived in 1943. Starting a home with few possessions, people gave her oddments and she bought items at Mr Walkey's furniture store in Osmonds Lane (now a night club) including a scrubbed wooden kitchen table. When the siren went at night, she carried her little girls down in blankets and crawled onto the single mattress under this table. In such frightening times, they cuddled up, listening to the thump of guns. Eileen's relief when it was all over was indescribable.

The council obtained white pine furniture from Scandinavia to issue to locals who had been bombed out of their homes, including Bob's sister in Myrtle Hill. Their mother suffered from a nearby bomb blast whilst visiting Mrs Rose in Higher Brook Street during the raid in September 1942. She became wheelchair-bound and Eileen had to care for her mother-in-law as well as both babies. She shopped at Marks Collins the Baker in Bitton Street and Carter's the Greengrocer on Fore Street. Supplies were scant and even dried fruit was not plentiful. Rowe the Butcher next door supplied her meat ration and on lucky days, she might get some offal or a couple of sausages from under the counter. White paper was wrapped around the meat and the parcel folded with newspaper, saved for this purpose by customers. Pulses, dried haricot beans, macaroni, spaghetti and Patna rice added bulk to meals. A grated apple or carrot in the cake mixture made up for the lack of sugar. She collected dried milk, orange juice and cod liver oil for her daughters from the WVS shop in Teign Street.

Bob served in the Italy campaign and was nearly grey when he came home in 1946. The long years away had disorientated him and he often slept on the floor. The family moved into a new two-bedroom prefab' at 68 Kingsway with a modern bathroom and kitchen. Christchurch, a nissen hut on the site close to the present Kingsway shops was used for Sunday worship and a community centre for Kingsway inhabitants. Parties and gatherings, and a social club for the men were organized. After seven happy years, the family moved to Third Avenue. Bob did several jobs, taxi driving for Owen Curtis at the garage adjacent to Shaldon Bridge and also in the cement works with Eric Phillips on Old Quay. He later worked for TUDC, driving a dustcart stored in the council yard on Quay Road, now a car park. Sometimes he drove the little sit-on sweeper along the seafront, but sweeping the corners in the shelters by hand. He served as a part-time fireman with Teignmouth Fire Brigade for 20 years. In 1988, Bob died of emphysema; his lungs shattered by desert sand and cement dust. Eileen lives in the town centre and continues to support the Salvation Army in memory of those two marvellous workers in Africa.

Coombe Road
Once a quiet backwater where the Aggetts lived, it was later renamed Coombe Vale Road. The car belongs to Mr George Whitear, a Brook Hill Junior School teacher.

Ruth I Johns nee Thomas

Writer, social innovator and community historian.

Our family moved from Hertfordshire to Teignmouth in 1938 when I was four-years-old and my brother four years my senior. My granny Martha joined us for safety some months later from Hythe, Kent. Her journey took twenty-four hours because all signposts had been removed, pending possible German invasion, in order to make it harder for the enemy. Our father Gilbert Thomas was a freelance writer and poet. Leigh Bank, the family home was on the steep part of Ferndale Road with splendid views of the sea, Ness and the Teign estuary. My mother's energies and skills were myriad and used to the hilt in our Teignmouth years. As it transpired, Teignmouth was no safer than Hythe. After France fell to the Germans, Teignmouth started to be bombed during daytime tip-and-run raids. Granny Martha refused to leave her upstairs room with its view of the Ness and died peacefully in her bed in November 1940 before the worst of the bombing, including night raids, took place.

Tip-and-run raids were notorious for planes dashing in from the sea, dropping their bombs and rushing out to sea, often before the alarm siren sounded. After a daytime raid, we would look over the town shrouded under a long-lasting cloud of thick smoke and dust caused by the bombing. Gradually people came up from the town and passed on names of any casualties. Leigh Bank was strafed on one tip-and-run raid. My brother, David, and I were playing in the garden. He looked up and saw the swastikas on gun-firing planes very near us overhead and yelled for me to lie down. I did and landed in chicken-mess, where a chicken pen had been moved to fresh grass. I disliked the result!

We spent many nights in the cellar. Planes returning from cities would sometimes circle round and round with a few bombs still to drop. Thus one night in 1941, the Hospital was hit. If adults felt fearful, they never showed it. As children do, I accepted that war was 'normal.' Armed sentries on duty on Haldon, and tanks coming down narrow lanes when we went for walks: these were facts of life. My only fear was that one or two of us might be killed in a raid when, during the daytime, all four were in different places. Being killed together was – for me – a better idea!

One or two evacuees were billeted with us and joined relatives already sheltering in Leigh Bank. One evacuee developed Chicken Pox. My mother, Dorothy, heard that the child's mother was also billeted in Teignmouth and contacted her, thinking she would wish to see her child. However, the mother said: "I might catch it" and kept her distance.

Early every morning, mother would go around our garden with a stream at the bottom checking that no German had parachute-landed overnight and, being injured, be unable to move. Gilbert was part of the ARP team that operated from Miss Marshall's house across the road. He was completely night blind and finding his way home in the blackout was difficult. Two elderly colleagues usually guided him down our gravel drive. During raids when we were in the cellar at night, an ARP warden came round to its door at garden level and shouted: "All right down there?"

Mother worked hard keeping morale high for all in the house. She organised homemade concerts and we all did a turn at singing, reciting or acting. The sitting room would be festively decorated, and simple homemade goodies appeared. Blackout curtains had to be carefully checked so that no chink of light escaped. Windows were criss-crossed with sticky paper to help prevent splintering if they were smashed in a raid.

View from the first floor of Leigh Bank, Ferndale Road, 1940
After a tip-and-run raid, the town was shrouded in a long-lasting cloud of thick smoke and dust.
Reproduced courtesy of Plowright Press.

We were fortunate in having an Ideal Boiler that produced enough hot water. Mother washed everything, including sheets by hand. She ironed, cleaned, stitched, knitted and mended, grew vegetables, bottled surplus fruit and salted surplus runner beans, made chutney and could cook a tasty meal from the most unpromising ingredients. She would walk over a mile to town most days to see what might be found on rations or points, and – with her two children – visit nearby farms for surplus fruit. It was sometimes brought home in a 3-wheeled barrow.

One night, my father heard distant bells when returning from ARP duties. Church bells were the agreed warning of impending invasion and my parents afterwards explained that they thought this was 'IT'. The next day, it transpired the bells were rung in Brixham and it was a false alarm. After Wheaton's 'went up' during an incendiary night raid on Exeter, our garden was littered with charred fragments from different publications. As kids, we were fascinated to read text clearly where the paper and print were in reverse, like a photonegative. Oddments included pieces from the Bible. Some nights we could see the glow from Exeter or Plymouth burning.

Teignmouth was not protected militarily and people who could leave were advised to do so. Our half-a-day a week gardener, Mr Bowden, and his wife were bombed out of their house in the town centre but they were not able to leave. My father was over fifty, could do his work anywhere, and so in 1942 our family evacuated at short notice to South Molton, taking only clothes and family photos. Mr and Mrs Bowden moved into Leigh Bank rent-free.

We returned in July 1944 when I was ten years old. Life back in Teignmouth resumed and I joined my brother at Teignmouth Grammar School. Due to my age, I had to sit the first-ever year of the 11+ examinations with two others. The others 'failed' and had to leave the school and that, for me, was an early introduction to what I perceived as injustice. Why should anyone 'fail' due to a silly exam result?

Morgan Giles Shipyard
Part of a Phillips cradle (L). The loft above the shed was known as the "Toy Shop". Morgan's Quay apartments replaced the shipyard in the 1980s.

Teignmouth harbour was a magnet for me. I boarded the cargo boats – often from Holland and Scandinavia – and cooked for sailors, posted their letters and chatted. I climbed into Morgan Giles' shipyard several times just after the end of the war and when it was still doing specialised work for the Admiralty. I worked my way along a narrow ledge of bricks holding on to what seemed a rather flexible corrugated iron 'fence'. Once I had reached the end, and some way out over deep fast-moving water, there was skill at turning the corner and working my way back inside the boat yard to see what was being built or repaired. Having done this several times without any problems, I was once spotted and a lot of shouting ensued. I was just around the inside of the end over deep water, and I knew I had to keep my nerve to reverse my progress safely. I didn't try again!

The need for this closeness to the shipyard had something to do with a 20-year-old cousin who lost his life as an apprentice in the Merchant Navy in 1942 whilst serving on an Atlantic convoy. I heard adults whisper about this but – as was usual then – children were 'protected' and thus my imagination ran rife. So whilst, early in the war, I experienced bombing without any special fear, my cousin's death at sea was something I imagined over and over again for many years.

Valiant in the harbour
Requisitioned and renamed Valiant by the Royal Navy, this craft flies a white ensign. Official records show that on 3rd June 1940, this motor tug and Heron were brought into Morgan Giles shipyard and made ready to sail to Dunkirk. Three Teignmouth boats, Britannia, Shamrock and Golden Wings and Meteor and Eclipse from Torquay were also prepared to cross the channel to help evacuate the British Expeditionary Forces. Only four vessels set off but none completed the journey. Valiant put in at the Isle of Wight to refuel and was ordered home.

A gift from the USA
Ann Hook at Ivy Lane with her father Bill (L) and grandfather William and a Panda Bear brought home for her by Uncle Syd, serving in the Royal Navy.

Graham Rowland

At the age of 9, Graham and his sister were brought to Teignmouth from Torquay in a sidecar combination on their father's motorbike. The beach was technically out-of-bounds but people could go on it at their own risk. Few people were around and after a time, when they were all seated on the sand together, his sister said, "Look at those seagulls". They all stared out to sea where some black dots were skimming low above the waves. Just as the dots became visible as planes, their father pushed them down and lay protectively across them. It all happened so quickly that they did not have time to become frightened. Graham had spotted the unusual wing shape of the handful of enemy aircraft and believed them to be Stuka fighter-bombers. Bullets from machine guns were heard, followed by the bumps and bangs of falling bombs and moments later, the planes went overhead and back out to sea. By the time they had gathered their belongings and were heading home, the town had come alive with Rescue Services and ARP wardens. People were being carried on stretchers from smoking buildings. Although Graham cannot confirm the dates, it is likely the raid was the one that took place at 5.30pm on Thursday 13th August 1942 when eight enemy planes delivered the town's 17th raid.

By the pier on west beach
A concrete anti-tank device shrouded in barbed wire helped protect the promenade. Marjorie Hexter of the WRNS takes her ease on the sands. The Hexters ran the tea hut on this site.

Derek Northcote

I attended Grammar School 1936-41. On 7th July 1940 my friend Tony Hill and I were on a sandbank a few hundred yards south of the pier when a twin-engine aircraft came out of the clouds and flew very low over us. We thought it bore French markings. We could see the crew and waved and they waved back. Then we saw objects flutter from the plane and soon realized that they were bombs. We both dived as deeply into the water as we could and surfaced to hear the sound of the explosions echoing around the area and the plane heading out to sea.

May Shorthouse, WRNS

May spends some off duty time on west beach. Two sections sliced out of the pier to deter invasion are clearly visible.

May Shorthouse and Leading Seaman Green

Dancing partners from the London Hotel, they are all smiles despite the rolls of barbed wire. May later married local seaman, Jim Day.

London Hotel Ballroom
Dances were held here almost every night during world war two. Cecil Kelly, playing the drums, and his band played there regularly.

Rita Menghini nee Boyne

Rita was born in Edinburgh in 1920. When she was three months old her family moved into Mulberry Street, Teignmouth. Her family were Navy orientated and she joined the WRNS - Women's Royal Naval Service at the recruiting office in the old library in Brunswick Street (currently a public toilet.) She was based in the former Marina Hotel with the Fleet Air Arm. Groups of pilots, about 15 at a time, were sent down from Yeovil, and later expanded to Yeovilton, for training at Haldon Aerodrome. Some of them towed the drogue for target practise and others trained as rear gunners. Rita recalls the dances at the London Hotel when servicemen and women packed the ballroom.

Margaret Day & Steve Upchurch wedding day at St Michael's Church
L-R: Rita Boyne, Cook at Marina, Cpl Arran, Joseph Charles Day, Alice Day
and her son Jim behind her with May Shorthouse and Sheila Day. Ida Smith
brandishes a rolling pin to signify Margaret's work as a cook.

Wedding guests
L-R: David Day, Nettie Grant, Cpl Arran, Ethel Beddows WRNS, Charlie - Bus
conductor, Sheila Day and Lil Harris, whose parents kept the Ship Inn.

Frederick Hook and family
Outside the Kings Arms, French Street in 1941. The baby is John, who followed his father and grandfather into Teignmouth Coastguards where he gave 43 years service before retiring in 2004. The Belgian Urn now stands on the Den.

Jill Reed nee Court

When war was announced, 10 year-old Jill was in bed with scarlet fever. The day was very hot and her father stripped to the waist, and dug up their lawn in Pennyacre Road to make way for an Anderson* bomb shelter. It remains there to this day. The family was evacuated to Ilfracombe but her father stayed on to work with Jill's uncles, Lionel and Reggie Broadbear. He was their partner in the garage business at 25 Regent Street. At 4pm on Wednesday 2nd September 1942, the brothers were hard at work in their inspection pit underneath a vehicle when suddenly, the 18th raid got underway without warning. Four enemy planes came in very low and each dropped a bomb causing 8 deaths and 33 casualties. The French family kept the Esplanade Hotel, standing only yards from the garage. It had a direct hit and the attached Berkeley Hotel was so badly damaged, it had to be pulled down. Although the hotels were used by numerous troops as a billet, nobody was in either building at the time. The Broadbear's dog Chummie had been blown down the road by the blast but soon reappeared at the garage. The brothers escaped without a scratch, presumably having been protected by the inspection pit.

*Anderson shelters, named after the Home Secretary, were small, arched steel and corrugated iron huts designed to be dug into the ground. They saved people from debris but not a direct hit. As war broke out, 1.5 million had been issued to people in perceived danger zones.

Florence Wood 1902-1985

Florence was sister-in-law to Harold Wheeler who was a teacher at Teignmouth Grammar School. She wrote this account to present to a Methodist women's group, many years after the event.

December 23rd 1941, the telegram boy was knocking at our door. With apprehension we tore open the orange envelope. It was from my sister in Teignmouth. Her father-in-law had died suddenly and her husband was going home to Suffolk. She and 2 year-old Heather would be spending Christmas alone. The family felt that someone should go down and spend Christmas there so I volunteered. It was dark when I set out on Christmas Eve for the 12-hour journey, going first to Huddersfield by bus. As I crossed on foot from the bus stop to the railway station, the trolley buses loomed out of the darkness, their tiny hooded blue headlights looking like the malevolent eyes of fearful monsters. Teignmouth seemed so very far away - like the end of the earth - as I shivered on the platform. I hadn't been on the train long when the dawn crept over the sky and the sun rose. There was plenty of room on the train and only three ATS girls going home on leave shared my compartment. It was a pleasant journey and the day passed quickly until the winter sun set and the light faded from the sky.
When we reached Exeter it was quite dark. My fellow passengers had left the train and I was alone. Suddenly, all the lights went out and as I hung out of the window all I could see on the busy, noisy station were swinging points of light from dark lanterns. One dancing point of light came swinging alongside the train towards me and as it drew level I addressed the shadowy outline of the carrier, asking when the lights would come on again. The light swayed to a standstill and a voice replied, "They won't come on at all, lady. The line from here to Plymouth is mostly visible from the sea and we can't take any risks." There was a banging of doors and a whistle and the train restarted.
It was as black as Egypt's night. I groped my way back into the compartment wondering how I was going to collect my scattered belongings. I couldn't

even see the outline of the window, eyes closed or open, it was all the same. I knew that quite near was the English Channel: there had been a number of raids and they were growing more frequent. After a time, the darkness seemed to become less intense. I found I could distinguish the faint outline of the window. Slowly it grew lighter and lighter until slowly a bright full moon crept over the horizon and flooded the compartment with moonlight. Through the window were glimpses of a sparkling sea. I gathered my things, put on my hat and coat and waited.

It was about 8pm when I arrived at Teignmouth and though it was so early on Christmas Eve, the streets were quiet, few people were abroad. I walked up Exeter Road between leafless trees that made a lacy pattern on the road. I stopped and turned to admire the scene below - the sharp silhouette of the church, the moonlit rooftops of the quiet town and beyond the shining sea. As I stood I heard the sound of music: choir boys out carol singing Holy Night, Peaceful Night. It was like awakening from a nightmare.

Brownies and Girl Guides
The group photograph, date unknown, was taken in Brook Hill School playground.

Report from Teignmouth Post, March 1943 when Lady Baden Powell visited Teignmouth Guides.

The Teignmouth guide company dating from 1911 was one of the first to be formed in Devon. During her tour of the county, Chief Guide, Lady Baden

Powell came to inspect them. The Sisters at Notre Dame Convent offered their gymnasium for the event. Companies represented were 1st, 2nd, 3rd and 5th Teignmouth, Bishopsteignton, Shaldon and the Lifesaving Guards of the Salvation Army. Guides formed a guard of honour with their standards and the Sea Rangers semaphored "Teignmouth welcomes the Chief Guide". Lady Baden Powell chatted freely with many members and gave the officers a hearty handshake. She expressed her delight at returning to Teignmouth, a place she had known years earlier. She was full of admiration for the way that people were "sticking it despite the worries and anxieties they were passing through" and referred to her "family" of over one million children worldwide through the guiding movement. Children of all shades, race and nationality were members of a sisterhood cemented by friendship and goodwill. This was something to think about in a world at war.

Sheila Robbins nee Skinner

Parents of Bishopsteignton 1st guides had to sign official dockets to allow us to attend meetings with Teignmouth 2nd guides (Grammar School) in St James Hall. The leader, Miss Allerton from Holcombe, taught us first aid skills. The guides were trained in semaphore in the school playing fields. Breaking into two groups, they took it in turn to signal across the field using pairs of blue and white flags divided diagonally. Miss Lynne trained pupils as Red Cross cadets. A parcel label was attached to anyone who was injured by an air raid, to assist with keeping the statistics of people who suffered injury.

Ken and Win Bennett

Growing up in Teignmouth, they recall brick bomb shelters dotted around the town. One stood in the centre of the wide section of road at the junction of Somerset and Northumberland Places. Win lived near Mount Everest in the Grammar School grounds when it was used as a hospital by American troops. Wards were set up in nissen huts erected down the side of the house. Win and her friends sometimes played in large wooden packing crates stacked behind the house. They had been used to ship food supplies and were full of wood shavings.

Telephone No. 14

Devon Constabulary
"E" Division.

TEIGNMOUTH 3rd July ___ 1942

The Bearer is Mrs Doris Emily Nettleton (Holder of National Registratio Identity Card No. WGCJ/320/2) of Devon Arms Hotel, Teignmouth, who is visiting Weston-super-Mare, for the purpose of visiting her parents Captain and Mrs Woodman of The London Hotel, Weston-super-Mare - which Hotel was destroyed by Enemy Action.

D.E.Martin
Sergeant No.17.

Police Permit

Mrs Nettleton, landlady of the Devon Arms Hotel in 1942, had to obtain a special pass to visit her parents after they were bombed out of their hotel in Weston-Super-Mare. Five weeks later, a bomb narrowly missed the Devon Arms and destroyed the Town Hall on the opposite side of Northumberland Place.

Grace Nicholls nee Seal

My family lived in a flat in Greenwich, southeast London and when the bombing started every night, Mum said it was too dangerous for us to stay so we were going somewhere safe in the country. I was 8 years old when I was evacuated to Teignmouth with my brother Charles (9) and sister Jean aged 4. We gathered up in a local school and were soon enjoying our first ever train journey. We were told we were going to the seaside, another first so we were excited. It was a long journey but eating our packed lunch helped pass the time. Jean and I were billeted with Mr & Mrs Phillips in Bitton Crescent. Their daughters Hilary and Gladys lived at home and the other daughter Lily lived with her husband Ernie and son Bernard Charles in Alexandra Terrace. Mr Phillips was blind and every day he went out alone, tapping his stick on the wall at Clay Lane and finding his way down to the quay. We enjoyed living in a house with a garden and settled down, attending the local school. We played in the park with Hilary and Bernard and had no idea why the seafront had scaffolding poles and were disappointed that they prevented access to the beach. On several Saturday mornings, I visited the house of a local artist who painted my portrait. She always gave me some lemonade and a sixpence but I have no idea what happened to the picture. Some soldiers in the park heard us talking one day and told us that they were from London too. Whilst we sat on the grass to talk to them, a low flying plane approached, firing its machine gun. We all covered our heads and lay very still. Nobody was hurt but we ran home, very scared as we didn't think things like that happened in Devon. Mrs Phillips told us we could no longer stay with them but would still be with someone we knew. Their son and his wife ran a hairdressing shop a few doors away and Charles and I were going to live with the wife's parents, Mr & Mrs Smith at 2, Gloucester Road. Jean would live with Lily and Ernie in Alexandra Terrace so we remained within the same family. Once again we settled down happily in our new homes. Mum and Dad brought our baby brother down to visit us and we were surprised that he had grown into a toddler. They were happy that we had settled but must have had mixed feelings that they never revealed. Dad was very busy in the Heavy Rescue Squad at home in London. Beryl and Greta Smith (aged 11 and 8) had two brothers called Jack and Dick but we did not see much of them. A family of three, called Taylor lodged upstairs in the house. Life went on as normal until the night of 2nd July 1942 when I was woken by my brother pulling my hair. " Wake up!" he said. "I'm going downstairs…I can hear lots of noise like bombs falling and guns." I went down in my nightdress but without slippers. Mr & Mrs Smith heard us and also came down but I am not certain if Greta and Beryl came too. Dick was home on leave from the navy and was upstairs with his brother and the lodgers. We had only been downstairs a short time when we heard a plane very low then the sound of metal scraping on metal. There was a loud bang and the lights went out, a second bang, a great whistling sound, and then crash! The house fell in on us as Mrs Smith tried to shield us. After that I could see and hear nothing. I called to Charles but got no reply. I seemed to be in a deep hole and knew I had to get out but it was pitch dark. I tried to climb out but got nowhere and began to cry. Then a man picked me up and asked my name. "I'm Grace Seal the evacuee, I live with Mrs Smith". He told me not to cry and said I was all right now. "But I've lost my handbag and it had sixpence in it!" I cried. The only injury I sustained was to my feet that were cut and full of debris. I did not go to hospital, instead he took me to a place that was either a safe house or a rest centre where they gave me a drink - it may have been brandy and milk. Later on Charles, thankfully also uninjured, joined me. We were told that Beryl and Greta were safe but that Mrs Phillips, her two sons and Mr Taylor, the lodger had died. Mr Smith died shortly afterwards. My memory is not very clear following this. My father came soon afterwards to take us back home to London on the train. We had no belongings left but were lucky to have lived to tell the tale. We were so sorry about those who unfortunately did not survive.

Extracts from

TEIGNMOUTH POST

Friday 1st January 1943
Fourth Wartime Christmas
How it was spent in Teignmouth

The ringing of church bells on Christmas morning gave the festival a little of its pre-war semblance. Those of St Michael's Church led the way soon after the time allowed and were followed by those of St James'. It was the fourth war Christmas but in the home circle, unrationed happiness and revelry prevailed, with thoughts of those relatives on duty "somewhere". Despite wartime conditions, everyone endeavoured to fulfil the wish of "A Happy Christmas" and in the absence of discordant air-raid sirens this was possible. At the Hospital the patients had a good time and every endeavour was made to make Servicemen feel at home. May the blessing of peace and goodwill be ours for the Christmas of 1943.

The attendance at the churches on Christmas Day was larger than usual and the congregation joined heartily in the singing of the carols. At St Michael's nearly 200 persons attended Midnight Mass on Christmas Eve. The crib and Christmas tree were again in evidence but the altar was not illuminated in consequence of fuel restrictions. Although the festivities at the hospital were not on such a large scale as pre-war days the patients spent a most enjoyable time. Col. Ralph Rayner MP again provided the Christmas tree in the hall and holly and evergreen were again conspicuous in the decorations. Although turkeys were somewhat of a rarity, this was not so at the Hospital where the bird figured conspicuously at the midday meal. As usual Dr D. Ross Kilpatrick and Dr JM Courtney saw to the carving and distribution and this was followed by the proverbial plum pudding. Residents were most generous in their gifts of fruit and other delicacies, and the happy smiles on the faces of the patients were evidence of the appreciation they felt about what was provided for their enjoyment.

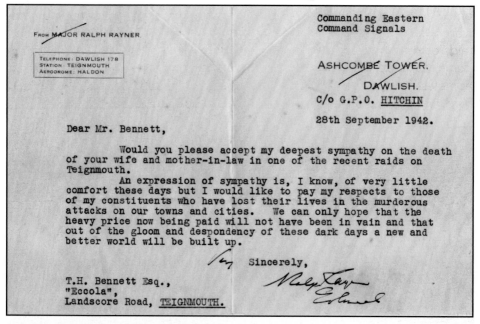

Letter from Major Ralph Rayner
Ken Bennett was playing with friends in Teign Street, only yards from his home in Albion Place when a raid occurred on 13th August 1942. He narrowly escaped injury but his mother and grandmother lost their lives and their neighbouring houses were totally destroyed.

CHAPTER 3

Doing their bit at home and abroad

Families split up.....armed forces requisition large buildings........the town is filled with people in uniforms....... Life changes forever.

Pride and patriotism pushed the public along through the dark days. Few families escaped anxiety about relatives and friends serving in the armed forces. Anthony Eden appealed for able-bodied men to assist in the defence of our shores from the imminent menace of invasion in 1940. Many men registered at the local Police Station and within days, hundreds of volunteers were drilling - but without any weapons. Squads of night watchers were based on Haldon to prepare for scores of highly organized enemy paratroopers that were expected to descend from the sky, bringing death and destruction. Air raids on the town took their toll of lives and property. Shortages of everyday items reduced living conditions even further. Many families rendered homeless had to squeeze in to live with family or friends. Despite tension and hardship, people did their best to dig their heels in and get on with it.

Home Guard, 1941
Local young and older men volunteered to defend the homelands. Training took place two evenings each week. The use of hand grenades was carried out at the assault course in fields near Labrador. Rifle practice took place on a range at Starcross.

Warwick Wingham Tapper 1909 – 1968

Warwick Wingham Tapper, the tall man in the back row of the photograph on the previous page was the eldest of five children in a well-established Dawlish family. At the age of 11, he was sent to live with his grandmother after the death of his father. Warwick became a furniture sales assistant at Jay's of Exeter and married in 1932. They moved to Teignmouth and opened a furniture shop at 25 Fore Street, some of the items sold then are still used in local homes. Jovial to his customers, he was strict at home and his baby daughter Joan had to sit in a high chair behind her father at mealtimes. He volunteered to join the Home Guard in 1940. The following year, he was recruited into the army and posted to Worksop, Notts. Standing 6'8", he had a uniform specially made for him and was granted double rations in accordance with his size! His wife took Joan and her sister Valerie to live with their grandparents in Exeter. After demob' in 1945, Warwick purchased a small shop in Higher Brook Street and stocked it with second-hand furniture obtained from auction sales. It was an astute plan since many people were seeking to replace belongings lost or damaged in air raids. Warwick enjoyed sports such as swimming, bowling, table tennis and snooker and won the Teignmouth Conservative Club snooker shield in 1955. Poor health forced early retirement and early in 1968, Warwick collapsed and died during a round of golf.

Mavis Hook nee Mole, 1941
Born in Shaldon in 1923, at 19 years old, Mavis joined the ATS - Auxiliary Territorial Service. After six weeks training at Denbury camp, she was transferred to the Royal Army Ordnance Corps at Wembley, the same regiment as Princess Elizabeth. Mavis was responsible for issuing stores to British and American soldiers including several famous film stars.

WRN Marjorie Hutchings nee Davis, 1941
At Alexandra Terrace.

Marjorie was born at 6 Alexandra Terrace in 1917, the first child of Henry Davis, a blacksmith working for J.Best, and Lilian Gourd, daughter of HD Gourd who founded the Bishopsteignton transport business. She trained in business studies at West Lawn night school and the Labour Exchange found her a position at Lendon the Butchers on Fore Street. In 1940, she married Fred Hutchings who was in a reserved occupation and they made their home with her parents.

Advised to join the WRNS, Marjorie went in as a writer and was trained as a telephonist by a GPO supervisor, becoming one of a team of 8 based at the Royal Hotel. She sometimes rode her bicycle to Newton Abbot to meet Fred and narrowly missed getting caught up in the raid near the gasworks at Broadmeadow on 13 August 1942. The shock of her close encounter gave her the impetus to ride straight up Bitton Hill without dismounting! She went to

the Riviera Cinema that night and the film was called "Hell's a'popping!"
One drizzly Sunday, she went on duty at the switchboard in the Royal at 8am. She was due to finish at 1pm but her replacement was late coming over from Shaldon on the ferry so Marjorie continued taking messages. A signal came in that all flying was cancelled - this meant that any planes in the vicinity would be enemy ones. Whilst her mother was serving up their roast dinner, a plane was heard. They rushed to the Morrison shelter on the ground floor and just as her father pulled his leg in underneath, an explosion occurred. Their own house, number 6 was destroyed as were 7, 8, 9 and 10 Alexandra Terrace. Their immediate neighbours in number 7, Mrs Pratt and her son George, home on leave from the Merchant Navy, were both killed. George's body was blown by the blast into number 6 and was found on top of the Davis family's shelter. They eventually managed to climb out through the window frame of their collapsed house. The bodies of five of their neighbours were laid out on the street and an Air Raid warden advised Marjorie to look away. She lost all belongings including precious photographs, except the one of her in uniform and another taken at her wedding. Fred said, "At least we've got each other". The Salvation Army was soon on the scene, serving hot, sweet tea and Marjorie supports them to this day. Incredibly, a month after the raid, their cat was found wandering about in the rubble and in time changed from skin and bone to a flourishing creature.

Marjorie was put up at the Marina Hotel at the end of Powderham Terrace, occupied by the Fleet Air Arm and her parents went out to stay with the Gourds. She removed to HMS Britannia II at Royal Naval College, Dartmouth, operating the communications underground and was made up to Leading WRN and transferred to the Fleet Air Arm. "I always seemed to be on duty when the big raids were coming....they used to call me Jonah! Although the war was a worrying time for us all, people were much kinder to one another then." She was hospitalised at Yeovil and did not see Fred for about a year then by strange coincidence they stepped off the same train at Teignmouth station - neither knowing the other was aboard. Reminiscing at 88, Marjorie's smile embodies the spirit of someone who saw so much heartbreak and knows far more than she will ever impart.

Maurice Louis Charles Mortimore 1916 - 1942

Maurice was a member of Teignmouth National Fire Service and was on duty at the Fire Station in Northumberland Place when a bomb destroyed it on 13th August 1942. Maurice, only 26 years old, was killed. The NFS was manned by females, mature males and younger men, deferred from active service because of their reserved occupations. Included were Harry Ware-Radford and Bill Matthews, who was on Morgan Giles workforce and became Station Officer in the 1950s.

The bomb-damaged fire appliance was rebuilt and put back into service. Its bell was saved and put on display in the entrance hall at Bitton House. In 2004, the Town Council agreed to my request to place a copy of this photograph of Maurice beside the bell. A new Fire Station is currently being built on Higher Brook Street.

Morgan Giles workforce
FC Morgan Giles kept about 150 people, men and women, in full-time employment at his Strand shipyard during the war years. All the windows of

the shipyard were blown out during the raid on 10th January 1943. A large amount of valuable stores were scattered across the street and the youngest son, Robin was stationed at the yard entrance to protect them. The significance of their contribution to the war effort through fulfilling the demands of the Admiralty will never be fully known.

Leading WRN May Day nee Shorthouse

May met Jim when she came to Teignmouth as a teenager on holiday from Wales. Eventually she got work here and in May 1940, she was accepted into the WRNS after being interviewed by a female officer in the Royal Hotel. Requisitioned by the Royal Navy, a top-secret communications centre operated from the basement. May was soon in uniform and based in the former Marina Hotel on the south end of Powderham Terrace. Other local girls in the Fleet Air Arm group were Jim's sisters, Sheila and Margaret Day, Rita Boyne, Jenny Swarbrick, Joan Hodge, Lil Drew, Ethel and Amy Beddall, Joan Palk and Monica Townsend. They worked in pairs and Monica partnered May. Their duties included preparing food, delivering and serving it to the servicemen, some of whom were based at Haldon Aerodrome. They were taught how to deliver a correct Royal Navy salute in the teachers' rest room at Brook Hill School and learned to march on The Point car park. She was rated up to Leading WRN. After six months May was sent to HMS Raleigh at Plymouth, stationed at Anthony House and was trained as a telephonist.

May and Jim were married at St Michael's Church in June 1942 and enjoyed a small reception in King William IV in Northumberland Place. They had a three-day honeymoon in Padstow, staying at the same hotel where Jim's father, Joseph booked in when he was fish dealing in Cornwall. He was very supportive to the young couple, paying for their honeymoon and after baby Alan came along, providing them with a home of their own above his fish shop in Teign St. Although the property had been damaged during an air raid, he had it done up for them. Every day he brought some fish for their tea and made sure they were all right. On Sundays at 11am, he took his little grandson out for a walk before enjoying his customary pint at the King William IV. A Belgian refugee came seeking a job and worked in the fish shop. Alice, May's mother-in-law provided him with a dinner every day, despite food rationing. Many years later, Jim and May visited him and were delighted to discover that he had made a success of his life in his homeland. May looks back on her time in the WRNS as very enjoyable and she really appreciated the comradeship and different lifestyle it provided.

Able Seaman Jim Day

Born Teign Street in 1920, Jim grew up at 2,Teign View Place. Six weeks after war was declared, he went to see Mr Goldfinch the Harbourmaster to find out how to join up. Jim was 19, about the same age as the group of friends who decided to go into the Royal Navy together. These included Roger Matthews, Bob Barge, Jack Riches, Les White, Bruce Sutton, Albie Nason and Bill Keyte of Shaldon. They boarded a train to Portsmouth and were soon training in the barracks except for Bob Barge who was colour blind and went instead into the army and later the Airborne Division. They soon got some experience at sea and the first real challenge came in May 1940 when the gang joined the crew of the converted paddle steamer *Medway Queen.* They knew their destination was Dunkirk but had no idea that they were to take part in Operation Dynamo. Hundreds of ships, large and small were used to evacuate thousands of the British Expeditionary Forces trapped on the French coast. Jim was a gunner in charge of a 12-pounder canon. *Medway Queen* got in as tight as possible to shore, then small boats ferried the troops out to the vessel, under cover of darkness and often under fire. A group of people attempting to fleé France had donned British uniforms in a bid to get out to the ship and some Spanish people were picked up on one of the trips. The vessel went over and back to Dunkirk seven times during the very hazardous week. Jim escaped injury but some of his shipmates were not so lucky.

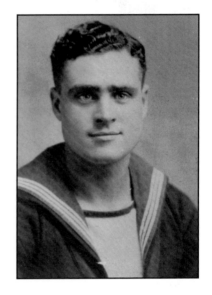

He later joined the *Conqueror* out of North Shields and was engaged in minesweeping in the Atlantic and home waters. For a time, *Conqueror* set out on her sorties from Dartmouth, sailing north of Ireland and out into the eastern Atlantic. The ship came under fire on occasions but Jim was again fortunate and escaped injury.

He has never forgotten the most harrowing element of the war which was at Dunkirk when they were forced to leave behind many injured servicemen who would inevitably have died in the water or on the beaches. His shipmate Albie took an injured man on board and was later reprimanded for his action.

Jim joined the Dunkirk Veterans Torbay Branch in the 1970s and was surprised to discover that the Chairman was one of the men rescued by the Medway Queen. For nearly 25 years, Jim and May paid an annual visit to Dunkirk to muster with the veterans and pay tribute to those who lost their lives.

Medway Queen White Watch on Flamborough sweep
Many Teignmouth lads who joined up together found themselves aboard this vessel.
Back row L-R: Bill Keyte, Jim Day, Arthur Maragar, Leading seaman James and Spot, ship's mascot.
Front row L-R: Albie Nason, Bruce Sutton, ? Walker.

Medway Queen at Dover, June 1940
The former paddle steamer has gone down in history for making more trips to evacuate our troops from Dunkirk than any other vessel, apart from a naval ship.

HMS Mount Stewart, Teignmouth shore establishment 1943 – 45

Commissioned as a combined unit, it consisted of servicemen from the Royal Navy, Royal Marines and Army specializing in irregular warfare. The Commander was Captain J Brunton RN who led approximately 35 Officers, 60 Ratings and 25 WRNS. Underwater swimmers were part of the team that operated from buildings on Eastern Quay and near Lifeboat House. The equipment used included folding surface canoes and rigid, mobile submersible canoes that were a similar size to a motorbike and sidecar. They ran on batteries and carried limpet charges. Another innovation was explosive motorboats, 12 foot in length. The craft were dropped with a driver inside and three parachutes attached, from Lancaster bombers. HMS Mount Stewart was paid off after VE Day. Some locals recall several small, unusual craft of this kind lying around in the council store at Gales Hill for years afterwards.

The harbour, where secret training was carried out

Fishermen's lamp at the Point

After Phil Nathan volunteered to join the RAF, his wife and two daughters kept his fish business going from the hut, beyond the lamp. They cleaned the catch in ice-cold water and boxed it up late into the night. Loads of fish, eight stones at a time, were pushed to the railway station in a wheelbarrow. The girls made deliveries to private houses at Holcombe, Shaldon, and Bishopsteignton on a pushbike. They had to leave the site when it was taken over by the US Navy.

Five Teignmouth Seamen, 1941

Frank Hitchen, Syd Hook, Frank Drew, Dick Smith (killed Gloucester Rd bombing) and a man with the surname of Austen.

Christmas Greeting, 1943

Robert Aggett, serving in the Mediterranean sent this cartoon greeting to his wife Eileen at home in Teignmouth. Douglas Chapple and helpers sent 625 little booklets containing good wishes for Christmas to the men and women of Teignmouth and Shaldon away serving in HM Forces.

Smugglers Inn, Dawlish Road, 1943
Peggy Carter, who worked as a ground hostess at Haldon Aerodrome in the early 1930s, saved this snapshot of Lillie Stead, Women's Land Army. Troops frequented the inn and a shred of a story connects it with secret communications, spies and even Lord Haw Haw.

Kenneth Jones

Kenneth (clarinet) was one of 18 musicians dropped from the 7th Devons Regimental Band at Christmas 1939 for being too young to serve. Go home and wait for call-up or reveal their true ages and be dispersed into other units, they were told. All, except one, decided to adopt the latter course. Kenneth went on searchlight duty and later joined a boat crew. All survived the war except the one who went home who was, ironically, later killed in action. Teignmouth recruits included Kenneth's older brothers Leslie (drums) and Alfie (horn) also Vic Ripley and his father Chas who both played several brass instruments. A territorial battalion was formed and during an 11-month stay at Chagford in 1942, as part of the Royal Artillery, they trained with 6 pounder anti-tank guns. The band practised over the stables of Chagford House and later at the Moorlands Hotel. Their meals were served in Moor Park Hotel where the NAAFI was based. Once a fortnight, the band Beat the Retreat in Chagford Square.

7th Devon Regimental Band at Chagford, 1942

Noreen Mardon nee Aggett

Born in Teignmouth in 1924, Noreen was playing tennis at Lower Bitton the day before war was declared, and saw trains pass by filled with evacuees. That evening, she and Lesley Marles helped deliver the evacuees to local addresses. Noreen helped the war effort by collecting for National Savings. Each Monday, she sold 6d saving stamps to all the householders in Pennyacre Road. Her father, TH Aggett operated a printing business at Caxton House, Lower Brimley but orders were slim so he became the Milk

Wedding in the Sudan, 1949 - Jack and Noreen Mardon of Teignmouth

Officer at the Food Office in Orchard Gardens. Noreen left school early to run the business and learned compositing, setting up frames and how to work electrically operated machines. She acquired the skills of a master printer but had planned to make a career of nursing. She became engaged to Jack Mardon, a boat builder at Morgan Giles before being called up into the army. The couple decided to work for the Church Mission Society in southern Sudan where they were married in 1949.

Mary Rawlings nee Glover, 1940

Mary Rawlings nee Glover was born at the Ring of Bells, Willey Lane in 1922. Newly married, she left her job at Price's Dairy in Teign Street to do war work in Park Street premises for Mr Cannon who also operated a wireless shop in Fore Street. The working day was 8am to 5pm and the rewards were slim. Mary was one of a handful of local women who prepared electrical leads and operated the machines but had no knowledge of how the products were used, other than it was to fulfil the requirements of the Admiralty.

Robert Aggett serving in Italy, January 1945

Robert, who later served Teignmouth Fire Brigade, is at the wheel.

Joyce Lane nee Ingram WRNS, 1944

Joyce worked in a newsagents' in Shaldon but her aunt encouraged her to apply for work in Morgan Giles shipyard. Warned by the Labour Exchange that it was "sweated labour" she took the job anyway, crossing to the yard via the ferry each day. Pay was 34 shillings for a 44-hour week starting at 8am and ending at 5pm daily and Saturday mornings. Mrs Woodley was in charge of the female workers including Kathleen Eggbeer, Doris Robbins, Pearl Sampson and Sheila Graeme. They worked on motor torpedo and motor gunboats and wore dark grey dungarees and a sweater. Harry Sealey, Alan Breeze and Cyril Coleridge drove home copper rivets through planks

whilst the girls were inside holding a 'Dolly' -a metal rod in place. The work was heavy but not daunting and they simply got on with it, without question. They did rubbing down with sandpaper and painting the craft in battleship grey. Joyce never saw FC Morgan Giles but Tom Vinson the Foreman sometimes shouted "Come on! Remember the boys at The Front!" It was a happy workplace and Joyce reflects that she would not have had such a job in peacetime. Soon after their arrival in 1944, US troops strolled around the yard chatting to everyone. Joyce spent the evenings at home in Shaldon listening to the wireless, knitting and reading books borrowed from Morton Woolley's private lending library. She volunteered to join the WRNS but was told they were not taking in any more. Call-up papers arrived on 6th June 1944 and after informing the shipyard, Joyce was sent for training at Mill Hill, London. Six months later she was working as boat's crew, shore-based at HMS Tormentor. She moved around on a small craft carrying messages, goods and servicemen from the landing craft moored at Warsash between Portsmouth and Southampton. She was proud to see one of Morgan Giles' boats up there on which she had worked. Two years in the WRNS had not furnished her with any qualifications for civilian life. Home on leave, Joyce was invited to experience her first sail in a dinghy by one of the chaps in the yard. As they reached the mouth of the Teign, it overturned and Jim Matthews took a boat out to rescue her.

Stanley Apps

Teignmothian Stan drove an ambulance and a "blood wagon" and cared for the wounded and sick during the North Africa campaign. After that, his unit went right up through Italy. He sent this photo home with the message "sorry cannot come in person but this is the best I can do at the present. Keep smiling," As with many servicemen, he did not share his wartime experiences with his family. He became a taxi driver and was well known locally for his great sense of humour.

Squadron Leader Leslie Bossom, 1942

Leslie joined the Air Force in 1940 at a Babbacombe Hotel, used as a recruiting centre. The initial three months training in Torquay included marching up and down the seafront. He was sent to Woodley Aerodrome near Reading to begin pilot training and after gaining his wings, was sent

home on leave. He was due to undergo further training to become a fighter pilot but whilst he was at home, a telegram arrived calling him back to Woodley where he was to become an Instructor because of his teaching experience in civilian life. For the next few years, he taught men to fly. He became a Squadron Leader and in January 1945, was posted to the Central Flying School at Hullavington where he instructed Instructors. Demobbed later that year, he returned in time to begin the autumn term in his teaching post at Teignmouth Grammar School. In providing these details, his wife Marjorie observed that Leslie would doubtless have queried his inclusion in this book since his war was humdrum and far from glamorous. He was known and admired by many locals and earned his place in history. Leslie died in 1997.

Extracts from
TEIGNMOUTH POST

In 1943

Sqdn Leader Clive Stanbury

February. Five months after being awarded the DFC, Sqdn Ldr Stanbury, grandson of THL Stanbury of Hazeldown House was awarded the DSO for services in the Middle East. When an aircraft crash-landed in the desert too far away from base to be salvaged, the whole under-surface of the fuselage was ripped away but Sqdn Ldr Stanbury flew it to base for rebuilding. "His untiring energy and will to win during the period of our withdrawal from the western desert inspired all personnel with whom he came in contact."

Able Seaman Alec Dodd

September. A gunner aboard the patrol ship Lady Philomena, Teignmothian Alec used a 4-inch to track an enemy bomber. He waited until it swooped in low over his convoy and fired. It was a direct hit and the plane dived into the sea.

Lt Robert Russell

September. Lieut Robert Russell, son of Mr & Mrs Bert Russell, of the Royal Fusiliers was awarded the Military Cross. He led his platoon in a battalion attack on a strongly defended enemy position north of Enfidaville. It was a steep and rocky ridge; the slopes were mine-covered and swept by mortars and heavy machine gun fire. They attained their objective and brought away many wounded soldiers under Lt Russell's "determined leadership and total disregard for his personal danger." He was the greatest inspiration to his men under the most trying circumstances.

Dr AJZ Vanstone of Mira Ceti, Newton Rd, Bishopsteignton

Dr Vanstone wrote about Protozoa, phosphorescence not unlike a small firework display quite commonly witnessed on the river Teign. Less than one twenty fifth of an inch across, Noctiluca Miliaris resembles tiny blobs of jelly. The organism assisted the Allies in Japanese waters by attaching themselves to a convoy of enemy ships, steaming stealthily towards its objective in the dead of night. These microscopic animals, with their "torches" turned on meant the convoy was spotted by a Flying Fortress that returned to base to report its sightings. On the morrow, the convoy was met by a strong force that administered the most disastrous defeat in that area to date.

Third Anniversary of Home Guard in May 1943

Some 1,700,000 belonged to the Home Guard across the nation at this time. Major H. Bigg-Wither DSO commanded the local unit, C Company of men from Teignmouth, Shaldon, Bishopsteignton, Stokeinteignhead and Maidencombe. Marking the third anniversary of their formation, they marched through the town with well-drilled precision, mobile units with cycles and stretchers bringing up the rear. Cllr Irish, Chairman of Teignmouth Urban District Council took the salute from the Royal Hotel and the company marched on to the Den, watched by about 1000 people. A display of proficiency with arms was given despite the lack of weapons, limited to a few air and shotguns. The event ended in time for people to attend devotionals.

Charles Templeton

The river Teign could have claimed Charles' life when he spent two never-to-be forgotten nights in the area as an Army Commando. He had volunteered at the age of 17 in January 1942 to avoid expulsion from school in Taunton. Just two months later he was injured at St Nazaire and spent three months in hospital. As soon as he was back on parade in the spring of '42, he was sent to a holding unit in Plymouth and received raid training with Marine Commandos at Lympstone. The troop of about 30 men was toughened up with a march down through Scotland and Wales to Mount Batten. They left Plymouth and headed for Teignmouth, ending up on the water's edge at Morgan Giles shipyard preparing to make a night swim across to Shaldon. They had Dennison smocks – a camouflaged light jacket that fastened between the legs and became a sort of air pocket to help keep them afloat. They stripped down to skeleton equipment of small pack and pouches beside The Mole - their name for Morgan Giles's wall. They scrambled through the barbed wire and entered the freezing water. On reaching the far bank, they had to fight their way through another mass of anti-invasion measures blocking the beach. Charles had a full-sized wooden replica gun in his hand

and the leader of the unit used a covered torch. They had been spotted by one of the Home Guard who yelled out "Some mad bu***rs are on the beach...call out the guard." Several guards turned up but only one carried a genuine rifle. The unit admitted they were on an exercise and had to run round the village so two of the Home Guard led the way. The unit re-entered the water but the tide had turned and it was very hard going. They swam blindly towards what they thought was Morgan Giles but in reality they were being carried rapidly towards the Point. A landing craft came to pick them up and bring them back to the Teignmouth side. A local woman heard of

their plight and brought a tray of hot faggots out on to the beach and her daughter, home on leave from the WRNS served hot tea from large kettles.

The unit had been instructed to live off the land but their attempts to get fish by stunning them with hand grenades thrown in the river were unsuccessful! A Police Sergeant who had seen service in the first war was sympathetic and told them to call at a particular farm on the way up, where they would be given cider. They slept rough for two nights with the dubious comfort of three old blankets at the foot of a hedge on land overlooking the Teign, possibly near Partridge's Farm on the edge of Little Haldon. The troop marched off to Lympstone's Marine camp and by the autumn were heading back to Plymouth to set sail for Alexandria in North Africa.

Charles returned to Teignmouth to stay for a few weeks in the autumn of 2004 and attended both the Armistice Recall and Remembrance Sunday.

The Matthews Family

William Matthews, Petty Officer

Bill, the eldest, joined the Royal Naval Reserve (RNR) in 1933 and was immediately called up at the outbreak of war. He served on a minesweeper *Snaefell*, one of the many paddle steamers converted because of their shallow draft that allowed them to sail in about two metres of water. *Snaefell* made many trips to Dunkirk then returned to minesweeping the North Sea, working mainly out of South Shields. She was bombed and sunk but Bill survived and joined a fleet sweeper *HMS Peterhead*. He became a Petty Officer, was posted to Freetown on the depot ship *Edinburgh Castle* where he saw out the rest of the war. He died in 1955.

Roger Matthews, Sub Lieutenant

Renowned as a rugby player, Roger represented Devon in 24 matches. The war cut short his sporting activities and he joined the navy in 1939 with a group of other local lads. Several of them were sent minesweeping in the North Sea on a converted pleasure boat *Medway Queen*. She joined the flotilla of seven paddleboats on 27 May 1940 for Operation Dynamo to collect thousands of troops stranded at Dunkirk. They came under heavy fire from German shore batteries and two of the boats were destroyed but the *Medway Queen* went over and back seven times. Official records state that she rescued 3046 men but in reality, the figure was closer to 7000 since she also saved survivors from the sinking *Brighton Belle*. Roger was promoted to Sub Lieutenant and joined the fleet sweeper *HMS Wedgeport*. He was an enthusiastic photographer and recorded many wartime moments that, in recent years, have been exhibited in the fund-raising exercise to get the *Medway Queen* restored. Roger died in 1989.

Fred Matthews, Morgan Giles machinist
Front row right, Royal Corps of Signals, Starcross

Fred was a part-time despatch rider and was called into the Royal Corps of Signals in 1939. He had worked as chief machinist in the sawmill of Morgan Giles shipyard. Before long Fred was recalled to his original post at the shipyard, probably due to the influence of his employer who had to meet Admiralty demands on the shipyard, at an all-time high. Fred's skill at preparing and sawing planks was more necessary to the war effort than being attached to the RCS. He is still going strong at 87 and lives at Wembury.

Len Matthews, Shipwright Third Class

Len was land-based as a shipwright at Morgan Giles shipyard engaged with vital Admiralty work. He was called up in 1941 and posted to Weymouth with Light Coastal Forces. After volunteering for active service he got a foreign draft and spent the next 3 years repairing MTBs and other vessels. He served in several places including Naples, Malta, Alexandria and Italy. He returned home via the Medloc scheme that used railways to transport 1000 servicemen at a time. Len still remembers the efficiency of the feeding arrangements for such large numbers en route. In the post war years, he worked with his father, Pixie, operating pleasure boats from the pier. He recovered from a serious stroke and now, at 83, enjoys life in Royal Court.

Jim Matthews, Petty Officer Engine Room Artificer

A victim of the first bombing raid on Teignmouth, Jim joined the navy in 1943 and served on anti-submarine frigates. He became an engine room artificer aboard the Captain Class frigate *HMS Aylmer*. Within 10 days of being aboard ship with the 5th escort group in the Western Approaches, he was involved in the sinking of a submarine after their radar picked up an enemy submarine sending weather reports to Germany. The group of 6, including a Woolworth carrier went full steam ahead and found the snorkelling sub'. Forming a semi circle, they opened fire. *HMS Bligh* picked up 32 enemy survivors. Whilst he served on *HMS Mourn*, he was on watch with a senior officer who was suddenly taken short and left Jim and two stokers in the engine room to keep watch whilst the group of six ships steamed on about one mile apart. *Mourn* was on the

outside flank and a torpedo hit her fore magazine, blowing away the whole of her front part. Jim heard a single explosion and realized it was ominous. Orders came through to go full steam ahead and in the confusion, the engine room came close to getting into hot water with a build-up of pressure. More than 100 crew of *Mourn* were killed and because the group had to go in pursuit of the U-boat, Carly floats were thrown to the 30 survivors. The U-boat escaped so they returned to pick up the survivors. Covered in sticky, black fuel oil, they were rushed back to Plymouth for hospitalisation where it took weeks for the oil to be washed from their skin. Jim stayed on in the navy until the beginning of 1947.

CHAPTER 4

1944 – They're over here!

Friendly invasion by The Seabees......the US Navy sets up a base at The Point........Teignmouth opens it's hearts and homes to the newcomers.

The tide of the war was turning when Teignmouth experienced a friendly invasion, early in '44. Suddenly, the town was packed with men who talked like film stars. Locals still say the Yanks pinched all the prettiest girls, some of whom married American servicemen. Their support as Allies was overtly appreciated and good friendships made, some of them lasting to the present day. They lived in former hotels all along the seafront and their open-handed generosity with sweets and tinned fruit was greatly appreciated. They even staged a Christmas party for the kids in the Den Pavilion. The ball games staged on the Den were a welcome diversion. A bout of infectious disease confined some Seabees indoors so, seeking a little amusement, they began throwing ten-shilling notes out of the windows to the children below. Phillip Stocker was a lucky recipient. Their stay here was not long-lived but their impact on Teignmouth was unforgettable.

Naming the day
This postcard was saved for 60 years as a reminder of the Seabees' time here.

Quonset huts outside Courtenay Hotel
Bruno bunked on the first floor, left. The photographer's uniform has USN printed on it.

Courtenay House, Den Crescent and the Den Pavilion
The balcony of one of the properties in Den Crescent provides an overview of the cookhouse with its tall chimneys, next to the Den Pavilion. The British Legion building at the far end of Den Crescent was used as the Army guardroom.

Courtenay House
The Galley Crew on the steps.

Sickbay
One of the buildings along the seafront was used for the Infirmary. On the blankets in large lettering is US NAVY in capitals with the words Medical Department further down. Various oddments, including a urine flask, are on the mantelpiece above the tiled fireplace.

Bruno's story

Bruno A. Petruccione of the 28th Construction Battalion US Navy- "The Seabees", a former Master-at-Arms and Seabees Reunion Chairman, has fond memories of Teignmouth and has supplied this unique collection of photographs taken here in 1944.

I was in Teignmouth with the 28th Battalion Seabees from May to August 1944. We were a good unit and at the risk of being immodest, good at what we had to do. Among the places we served are Scotland, France, Iceland and Okinawa. I was one of the younger ones; many of the others have already passed on. We enjoyed Teignmouth and before leaving for France, I spent part of every day in the Den Pavilion that served as our mess hall. As the Master-at-Arms (Internal Policeman) in the galley, I ran the work crews. I bunked in the Courtenay Hotel across the street from the British Legion HQ on Den Crescent where I spent a couple of hours of D Day. I recall having some dances on the pier, the walkway to which had a large hole. We made temporary repairs to it. We also spent some time in the bar of the London Hotel and the King William IV. We introduced cold beer to Teignmouth and I also paid for a lot of it for some dart-playing pub sharpies! The pubs opened at 11am and closed at around 2pm then re-opened from about 4 to 9pm. We had ice cream machines and the Chief thought it would be nice to treat the children…that worked well for the first Sunday. The crowd grew with each succeeding Sunday with the addition of older children and parents. One Sunday when we had no ice cream powder, in true Seabee ingenuity and negotiation, we served strawberry shortcake. Those strawberries cost us a lot of cigarettes.

The first Sunday after we arrived, I wandered about the town in my dress blues and a gentleman invited me into his house for afternoon tea and some cookies. At the time I hated tea but he and his family were gracious in sharing what I am sure were made from rationed items. Unfortunately, I could never find that house again. A young lad who hung around the galley and ran errands sometimes sang, "There'll always be an England" and we would add…."as long as there's a USA!". He was a good kid and if he's still around, he can credit his longevity to me feeding him properly in 1944! We played football and softball on the Den, sometimes against some townspeople. One softball game was to benefit the local hospital, and to our chagrin, we lost.

I have a wooden plaque bearing the logo of the 28th and I will forward it to you to put in the Carlton Theatre. It should hang somewhere and we would be pleased if Teignmouth would do us that honour. I had then and still have, a lot of respect for the British people's courage, determination and resourcefulness in what were grim years.

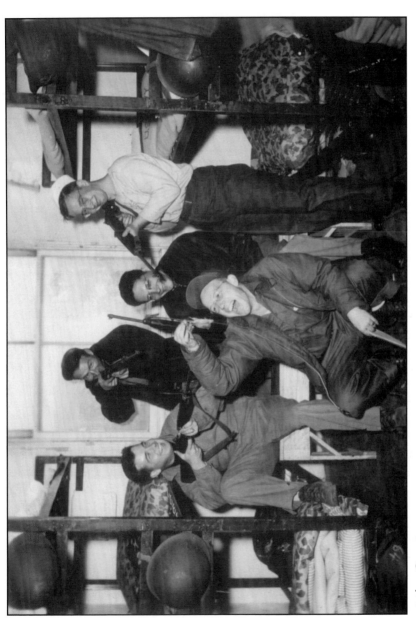

A bunkroom at the Courtenay

Some of the guys mugging with a mouse they caught. Clockwise from the guy in front of the window: Czajkowski the Storekeeper, Kaplan a Yeoman, Wilson the photographer who took most of this collection of photographs and currently runs a successful photography business in Ohio. Finally, Halen the Surveyor.

Quonset huts on Courtenay Terrace
Larger than Nissen huts, Quonsets were prefabricated huts of corrugated iron, having a semi-circular cross section.

Ball game on the Den
Over a hundred people gathered to watch the game. This may have been the one between the Seabees and a local team to benefit the hospital. A military truck is parked to the left of the Royal Hotel entrance.

The Den Pavilion from Courtenay House
The Seabees used it as a mess hall. On the far side of the Den is a sort of bunker near the present crazy golf site. Large vehicles are lined up close to the lighthouse.

Den Pavilion and cookhouse
Tall chimneys poke from the top of the cookhouse, erected next to the mess hall. The overview from a balcony in Den Crescent includes a brick bomb shelter on the left hand side of the picture.

"Holding down the beach head" at Teignmouth
The sun deck is festooned with barbed wire and a British sailor stands to the left of its right-hand pillar. A small boy, who must be local, sits crossed-legged near the servicemen.

The Pier
The Seabees bridged the gap in the walkway, cut early in the war to deter invaders, and held dances in the ballroom with its castle-like entrance of the late 1930s.

Interval refreshments served at the dance on the pier
Locals were treated to ice cream and other goodies at a dance. Bruno, far left with an eagle on his sleeve, was on Shore Patrol duty.

King William IV

Mrs Nettleton moved from the Devon Arms to take over the "King Billy". A poster, left, displays the current programme at the Riviera Cinema and another promotes full strength cocktails including Manhattans. Mrs Nettleton later used this photograph in the holiday brochure to attract visitors to the "Billy" as it was fondly known. It is now F&R's.

The bar at the King William IV
Vases of flowers gave the place a homely feel.

Mount Everest

Mount Everest became the Seabees' military hospital. Formerly named Trevervan, it was adjacent to Exeter Road. In later years, Bill Woolstan a caretaker was told that some of the US servicemen carved their initials in trees close by. Win Bennett nee Shemwell recalls a line of nissen huts along the driveway up to the house. Her father purchased a Daimler from Mr Ballard at a house sale just prior to his departure and the troops moving in. Demolition of the building coincided with completion of this book in 2005.

Outside Mount Everest
Seabee Medics at the impressive front door.
L-R: Stone the Dentist, Jones the Surgeon and Webb the General Practitioner.

Bank Street, 1944
F.W Woolworth & Co Ltd was known as the 3d & 6d stores. Neighbouring stores include Hepworths, International and Roberts the Tobacconist.

Over the rooftops from the back of Courtenay House
The rear of the buildings lining Little Triangle show years of neglect.

Teignmouth Invasion. 1st May 1944

Seabee, Bruce Caryl memorialised all the battalion's "visits". A large sign advertising Bovril appears on the wall to the left. Local girls have been glamorised into the typical all-female pin-ups of the time.

The Den bowling green
A relaxing game of bowls was an antidote to wartime stress and the club continues to flourish.

Near Lifeboat House
Land to the right was used by the US Navy to repair boats. A detailed diagram is included in Teignmouth at War Book 1. Americans likened the Ness to Diamond Head in Hawaii.

Overview from Courtenay House
The circular object on the Den was one of several water storage tanks dotted about the town and local boys sometimes took a dip in them. Den Crescent consisted mainly of hotels at that time, but none survived into the 21st century.

Galley crew at Cherbourg
Bruno, Master-at-Arms, is in the second row back, fourth from the right, wearing a chef's hat for fun. In the front row, 3rd from the right is Chief Flanagan, a fleet flyweight boxing champion from World War 1 who ran the operations at the Den Pavilion and gave ice cream to local kids.

Teignmouth Publicity brochure
This publication, issued through the Enquiry Bureau was included in the package of photographs that Bruno sent over. Saved for 61 years, it is in mint condition.

Eric Searle

I remember the Den Pavilion being used as a dining hall by the Yanks and many local kids, myself included, having meals there with the Seabees. All down one wall were big paintings of semi-nude girls, one of them adorned with an earring made from a crystal drop taken from a chandelier. Next to the Den bowling club another big nissen hut, with tall smoke stacks, was their

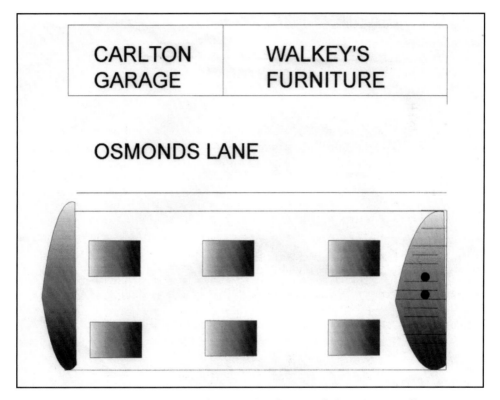

CARLTON GARAGE   **WALKEY'S FURNITURE**

OSMONDS LANE

US Navy Ablutions Block on the bombed site of the Town Hall

cookhouse. Most of us had our own adopted Yank and we got our Mums to wash and iron shirts for him. In return we got sweets, gum and sometimes a big tin of peaches and ice cream - a real treat then! The Yanks put another hut for ablutions on the site of the old town hall, bombed in 1942. It was next to Osmonds Lane, known as Walkey's Lane then because of the furniture store that operated where the nightclub now runs. Nissen huts in the car park of the Courtenay Hotel were used to store US servicemen's weekly ration of sweets, chocolate, gum and Lucky Strike fags. There was always a crowd of kids asking, "Got any gum, chum?" Towards the end of the war, the hut housed a Buzz bomb "doodle bug" and it was put on view to the public.

A Brief History of the US Navy 28th Naval Construction Battalion by Bruno Petruccione

Commissioned in Virginia in September 1942, the unit went within two months to Iceland to build an airfield at Keflavik. It was the largest airfield in the world at that time and its purpose was to provide air cover for convoys going to Europe and to provide a refuelling station for fighter planes being ferried to England. It was considered sufficiently important to give it Number 2 priority in the world, second to the African Front. The airfield is still used for military and commercial flights.

Late in 1943, The Seabees moved from Iceland to Scotland, to England and back to the States aboard the *Aquitania*. In spring 1944 they sailed on the *Queen Elizabeth* to Roseneath, Scotland and from there, moved around between Plymouth, Falmouth, Dartmouth and Teignmouth. The Headquarters Company of about 120 men was based at Teignmouth together with a US Army Coast Artillery detachment. The Seabees went on to France, some of them taking part in D Day at Utah and Omaha beaches. Together with the rest of the battalion, they restored the ports of Cherbourg, Le Havre, Brest and other places and in Paris they restored telephone communications. In late 1944, they returned Stateside before moving on to Okinawa and were at sea on VE Day. At Okinawa, the Seabees were a pontoon barge unit, similar to the Rhinos that were publicised in the Normandy Invasion. After VJ Day, the Battalion was broken up by discharges and through some being sent to China and Japan. The 28th included many men who were masters of their trades when they enlisted and the average age was 34 years... "old" for a military unit. It was the only world war two Seabee unit to make three tours.

Bruce Caryl, a commercial artist in the unit, designed a plaque and the men of the unit made five of them, using very basic tools. The motif reflects the airbase endeavour at Iceland. After making the rounds at annual reunions, it is now in their old mess hall, the Carlton Theatre, Teignmouth. It was unveiled on 21st August 2005 by Harry Sealey, who worked alongside the US Navy as a boat builder in Morgan Giles shipyard.

Seabees plaque unveiled in the foyer of the Carlton Theatre, 2005
L-R Roger Smith-Teignmouth Players, Harry Sealey, Teignmouth's Mayor and Mayoress, Cllr Geoff and Mrs Linda Bladon

Pauline Seaton nee Rose

I maintained correspondence with George Will, a US serviceman for over half a century. His letters invariably arrived with messages of good will to British people written in capitals on the outside of the envelopes. " God Bless the great people of England – my second home in 1942, 43, 44 and 45." Also "Happy Holidays to the brave people of England. You are all in my heart, after 50 years and Merry Christmas to my friends in Teignmouth. "

Extracts from George Will's letter

George was an American serviceman. Stationed here in the war, he made friends with Pauline Seaton. Half a century later, his letter to Pauline included this:

"It is 50 years since the war started, for us when we were shipped over to England. I have a great respect for the English people and feel that I am partly English. Never will I forget their kindness and friendship, especially the Rooke family in Teign Street. There were no braver people on earth and they shared what they did not have to share. Too bad people cannot live that way in time of peace. Sometimes I dream what a great treat it would be if we could all come together again and break bread in "Silent Concord" but we must content ourselves with at least our memories. I remain your friend and that of England. May God bless your great country and its people."

Sunset over the river Teign

CHAPTER 5

Happy & glorious!

*Peace comes.....members of HM Forces return home to build new lives......
rationing continues... ....Coronation of Queen Elizabeth II in 1953.*

Victory in Europe, announced on 8th May 1945 gave rise to thanksgivings and celebrations. Street parties prepared for children turned into a never-to-be-forgotten time of extraordinary levels of happiness. But out in the East, our troops were still fighting and victory was not achieved until 15th August. Even then, some servicemen and women did not return home for a considerable time. Teignmouth was bruised by 22 air raids and shocked by 79 deaths. Houses and streets were almost unrecognisable to those returning home after a long time away, serving King and country. Most of the large hotels on the seafront, occupied by troops, were being sold off for as little as £350. Assistance to purchase was provided for those intending to re-open hotels and help the tourist trade catch up on six years' losses. Teignmouth Urban District Council formed a Reconstruction Committee and appointed a town planning consultant to outline plans for a new-look Teignmouth.

Home Guard
Men of the local unit march through the Triangle on the way to the Den for the Thanksgiving Service in May 1945.

Teignmouth Red Cross
Nurse Audrey Lynne leads the women of the local branch.

Thanksgiving Service on Den
Thousands of people gathered to watch the arrival of marching groups from all the armed services and affiliated civilian groups.

Women's Royal Navy Service and the Sea Rangers

Women of the WRNS stationed at Teignmouth assemble with local Sea Rangers in front of the Royal Hotel

Dignitaries gathered on the bandstand

Names include Rev Wyatt, Cllr Irish, Rev Westall, Jack Price, Peter Mole, Dick Broad, Derek Paddon, Alf Underhill, Vernon Mole, John Armstrong, Tim Underhill, John Moore, David Orsman, Colin Panter, Colin Ingram, Paul Westlake, Jim Winsborrow, and Michael Gooding.

Reverend Westall and his wife, newly arrived in Teignmouth, handed out presentation wallets containing a ten-shilling note to all servicemen and women.

Victory Party on the Den

Hundreds of local children were seated at trestle tables set out in long lines for the official tea party.

Syd Hook DSM and his wife, Mavis, 1945

Early in 1945, Syd was given special permission to leave his duties and go to

Buckingham Palace to receive his Distinguished Service Medal. His mother and his wife Mavis accompanied him. King George VI presented him with his DSM and asked what he had done to earn it. Syd answered loud and clear in a rich Devon accent "Us got a clout, sir!" – it made the King chuckle! No official photographs were taken in the Palace courtyard and the only visual record of Syd's national recognition was snapped in the garden at Wembley. The couple met up briefly on 6th August, the day the atom bomb was dropped and recognized that the end of the war was imminent. Sixty years to the day afterwards, that moment remains a strong memory in Syd's mind.

The Matthews Family
Reginald Joseph Matthews known to all as "Pixie" with his wife, Emma Susannah, nee Belton. Their five sons served in, and survived, world war two. The family gathered at home in 2, Strand at the end of the war.

Britannia II
The Matthews' pleasure boat, dressed over all to mark her first trip out after the war.

Matthews' pleasure boats

Jim worked his father's pleasure boats, *Sea Hawk* and *Britannia*. The latter, built by Bill Bulley was renamed *Hindustan* by the Royal Navy. The River Patrol used the vessel to protect the harbour and to pull the boom across the estuary each night. She currently serves as a ferry between Turf Lock and Topsham on the river Exe. One winter, at the end of the 1960s, Jim was night trawling off Teignmouth with Jack "Snacker" Hook when their trawl got caught on the seabed. It took two hours struggle with the winch to pull free. They found themselves towing a Focker Wolfe wing piece, about 16 feet long by 5 feet wide. It surfaced on the way in, so they hauled it in tight after coming in over the Bar. It was 3am before they moored up in the darkness, bringing the wing up on the beach. In daylight, they found a cannon still embedded in it so Jim stored it in his hut. He sold it to a collector who restored it. The MoD made him return it to the seabed. The sand began to swallow the wing and within a fortnight, it was totally buried. In the summer of 2005, two attempts to recover the wing ended in failure.

Stanley Street
Eileen Wells nee Barnes on the spot where pretty little gardens now flourish.

VE plus 1, 9th May 1945
Girls' Friendly Society at "Le Chalet" celebrating. They founded the Service for Others' Committee soon afterwards. Back row L-R: Alice Cross, Mary Collins. Third row: Kath Lacey, Olive Dayman, Oriel Neville, Freda Hammond. Second row: Unknown, Nellie Russell, Audrey Sharp, and Muriel Bowden. Front row: Irene Hammond, Kathleen Warne.

Bitton Park Road
Many corners of the town remained in poor condition for a long time after the end of hostilities.

Heather Wheeler

Heather Wheeler (R) and sister Rachel
On VJ Day, 15th August in the garden at Thornley Drive.

I was born at Alwyns, Barnpark Road in May 1939. Our house, at the top of Thornley Drive was built in 1938. My father may have anticipated the coming hostilities as we had a trap door leading from the dining room to the cellar for us to retreat through during air raids. Years later, half-burned candles and an armchair were still down there. We also had a cream-coloured Morrison shelter in the sitting room but I don't remember being in it. My father kept chickens in a run on a narrow strip of land at the end of the garden below the house, and shared the eggs with Mr Paton, our neighbour. I enjoyed going to feed the hens with kitchen scraps. We preserved eggs for the winter in white paste-textured isinglass in big stoneware jars, stored in the cellar. Our Austin 7 spent most of the war in the garage but I recall a trip to Dartmoor for bilberry picking when my efforts were not appreciated after I was found putting rabbit droppings in the box!

As a master at the Grammar School, my father was in a reserved occupation but he had responsibility for deploying evacuees to work on local farms. A siren was situated on the school roof from where he did fire watching. The siren was retained for use as a fire alarm for many years. An alert sounded once when my father and I were passing the entrance to Lorris Drive so he pushed me through an old gate, into the hedgebank and protected me with his body.

The nearest bombing to us was at Yannon Drive and I played on the bombsite and picked winter heliotrope that was colonizing the rubble. The Blackout at our windows was a greenish-black material, and years later, a piece was used to make a shoe bag for me when I started at the Grammar School. Goods made during the war carried the utility mark and were not expected to meet pre-war standards. My father showed me a large, yellow fruit just after the war, and asked what I thought it was. I blurted out "banana" though I knew very well it was not. Fyffe's advertisement in a fruit shop window along Bitton Street had caught my imagination and it was wishful thinking that made me mis-identify a grapefruit! My sister Rachel, born in January 1944, was old enough to sit up in her high chair in the garden and, unaware of victory in Japan and wave the union jack signalling the end of the long war.

Badge 1939-1945
Teignmouth & Shaldon Thanksgiving Week, November 10th to 17th.

Victory party at French Street, May 1945
The tea tables, laid end-to-end are adorned with tablecloths and vases of flowers.

The Triangle
A quiet day in the post-war period.

Dick Roberts

Shaldon-born in 1924, Dick served with the Royal Artillery in many countries. In March 1946, after more than 3 years abroad, he was back beside the river Teign in Milford Park, as a Bombardier in charge of a Prisoner of War camp. As the commanding officer, Dick had one Lance Corporal to share the responsibility for around 150 German prisoners. A collection of army nissen huts, each with twenty bunk beds had been erected on the old tennis courts. The camp had shower blocks, hand basins and flushing toilets. The PoWs stood to attention for Dick who remembers them as pleasant and well disciplined. Several were middle aged and had not wanted the war any more than we had. They were industrious by nature and none of them attempted to desert. They were put to full-time work as labourers, some involved in the ground works for the 100+ prefabricated homes erected at Kingsway. Others were taken by army transport to a stone quarry at Brixham. The old pavilion,

Land next to Milford Park on Sunday 6th October 1946
Front row right, Bombardier Dick Roberts and his Lance Corporal on the left.
The man in the centre of the front row and others are German PoWs, still held
here 17 months after Victory in Europe.

once used by the tennis club, served as a dining and games room. Three of their own cooks prepared food in the cookhouse using Army supplies delivered from Poltimore House, near Exeter three times a week. They spoke little English and relied on their own interpreter. Four young Nazis were kept separate and made to do camp fatigues. The others were well behaved, obedient and respectful. Whilst waiting re-patriation, the PoWs were later granted a degree of freedom and every Sunday, Dick marched them down to the evening service in the Baptist Church. Tom Radford then in his teens sometimes helped escort them and says that the PoWs had to walk in the gutter, not on the pavement. Even in their spare time, the prisoners kept busy making dolls with a set of clothes, wooden wheelbarrows and mechanical toys.

Mr Curtis, who ran a garage business adjacent to the camp, was kind to the men and some worked for him. He allowed them to put a selection of their hand-made items on sale there. The PoWs created a garden at the rear of his garage. Mr Lee Edwards, Clerk to Teignmouth Urban District, invited them to tea in groups of two or three at his house overlooking the rugby ground. They always enjoyed watching rugby matches and played tennis and cricket when they got the chance. Dick was based there for 14 months until his de-mob in July 1947. The camp was closed within a month and the PoWs returned to Germany. Mr Milford bought the site and donated it, together with a cheque, to the council for use as a children's playground. South West Water encroached on this land in the 1990s.

Bombardier Roberts (R) and a Lance Corporal
Dick holds a puppy and his colleague, a kitten as they pose by the rear wall of Curtis's Garage that traded opposite the foot of Mill Lane.

Susan Morgan Edwards

German prisoners of war worked on land owned by her family at the top of Breakneck Hill. One, by the name of Ernst stayed on there to work for many years, living in a flat over the garages.

Modern life in a Prefab
Over one hundred prefabricated homes were placed at Kingsway in 1946. It took four days to build each unit. Nationally, a total of 156,000 were erected.

Teignmouth's new ambulance, 1946
Audrey Lynne (centre) was awarded an MBE for her work with Belgium refugees taking shelter in Britain during World War 1.

Regent Street
The Triangle, centre, is seen on this postcard sent by Rev and Mrs H Wyatt to Audrey Sharp at Christmas 1946.

Fred Niblett at Teign Street after de-mob

Pictured with his nephew Roy Geary, Fred's service in the Navy is over at last. Close to the Niblett's home, a WVS shop in Sun Lane doled out concentrated orange juice, one bottle per child per week, and dried milk to mothers. Betty Vickers nee Bace remembers that people had to get stamps from the Post office in order to be issued with the products. She loved the delicious wartime Spam in round tins.

George Robbins, Army Medical Corps in Nathanya, 1947

George, a Teign Street boy, was called up in 1947 and served with the Army Medical Corps for four years. He witnessed many atrocities as an ambulance driver in Palestine. When he finally returned in 1951, he was met at Teignmouth Station by all his family who then walked home together as a happy throng to 26 Teign Street. George died in March 2005.

Sheila Skinner, Ivy Robbins and Michael Robbins

Ivy Robbins, Michael and George's mother, bred budgerigars in her garden at Teign Street. She spent many wartime hours washing and ironing shirts for servicemen. She is pictured with her youngest son Michael and Sheila, who married her middle son, David in 1953.

Station Yard, 1947

The worst winter ever recorded compounded the hard times that people had to endure in the post war period.

Den Bowling Club, 1948
Cyril Carr was serving with the RAF when he arrived at Teignmouth. He married Pearl a local girl, and was later employed by the Urban District Council.

West Lawn School Football team, 1948
Bryan Back holds the ball for the group photograph.

Bitton House, 1948
Cllr Davidson handing out Australian goods to Teignmouth's elderly people.

Promenade on Easter Monday, 1949
The Weekes family L-R: Robert, his mother May, and wife Maureen, and father, Guy. David is in the pushchair beside Tatty the dog.

Fire appliance registration number CTT 45, in Carlton Terrace
This appliance was a Pump Wheeled Escape. After being damaged when the Fire Station was bombed in 1942, it was returned to its makers and was rebuilt, ready for another stint of service. The Police Station was built on this site in 1967.

Fire at the Carlton Cinema, 1951
When the fire occurred, the film of the week was The Forest Rangers.

Teignmouth Fire Brigade
Winners of the Best Station in 1952/3/4. The appliance was a Commer Water Tender.
Back row L-R: Percy Winsborrow, Walt Nethercott, Albert Roe, Reg Perryman, George Wise, Arthur Jones, Ted Clode, Dennis Sibthorpe
Front row L-R: Bill Holland, Jack Strong, Jeff Gale, Bill Matthews, Jack Phillips, Fred Passmore, Ken Jones.

Near the Lighthouse, 1949
Val Sharp, aged 3, rides a MoboBronco.

Teignmouth Hospital foundation stone
Dr Ross Kilpatrick laid the stone on 19th March 1953.

The Knight Family, 1953
When they lived at Mount Everest, the approach was enhanced by a rose garden

Grammar School sports field, early 1950s
Mr Knight, the school groundsman, cutting the grass above the tennis courts.

Teignmouth celebrates the Coronation of Queen Elizabeth II on 2nd June 1953

Celebration programme

Alice Cross and her supporters arranged a dinner of Heinz Tomato Soup, cold meats, boiled potatoes and garden peas, followed by fruit jellies or trifle and tea. Entertainment was provided by Teignmouth Follies, Barbara Spencer Edwards School of Dancing, Neta Drew School of Dancing, Pat & Beryl Adams (Comedy duettists) Tony Sutton (Magician) Rosie Rutter (Soprano) and Accordionist, Leslie Head.

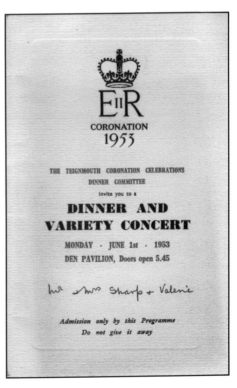

CORONATION
1953

THE TEIGNMOUTH CORONATION CELEBRATIONS
DINNER COMMITTEE
invite you to a

DINNER AND VARIETY CONCERT

MONDAY · JUNE 1st · 1953
DEN PAVILION, Doors open 5.45

*Admission only by this Programme
Do not give it away*

Celebrations
This party took place close to Headway Cross.

Richards' shop in Brunswick Street
Val Sharp stands in the doorway of her grandparents' boot and shoe repair shop with its window dressed to mark the occasion.

Children's Fancy Dress Parade
The event was staged in the Rugby Field.

Crowning Glory
The Triangle toilet block dating from the 1920s was topped with an impressive crown of lights. The building was demolished in the 1990s.

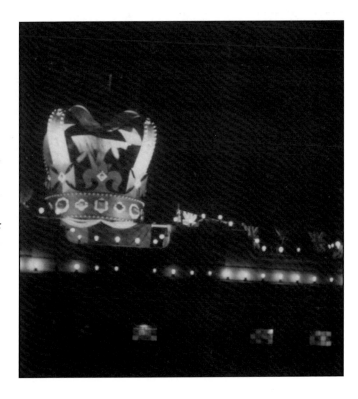

Fire Station party
All the children living in The Avenues attended a Coronation party. Family names include Turner, Carpenter, Northcott, Hooper, Passmore, Taylor, Jones, Cousins, Vicary and Evans.

Floral Tribute
Mr & Mrs Hooper marked the Coronation by planting flowers to form E"R in their front garden at Coleman Avenue.

Children's party in French Street
Triangular hats with a union flag design and advertising a well-known brand of tea are worn by several children of the 30+ children gathered around the table.

Hermosa House Lawn
Hermosa House was still being used while the new hospital was being built on Mill Lane. On Coronation day, people dressed up and played cricket and other outdoor games.

Hutchings Way celebrations
A dog called Scamp takes centre stage at this Coronation party.

Cartwright Crescent party
Fireman Arthur Jones took this happy group, his wife Ruth is sixth from the right of those standing.

Coronation Boat
Festooned with flowers and bunting, it was photographed near Morgan Giles shipyard sheds on the evening of Coronation day.

Brook Hill School
Pupils were given Coronation mugs to commemorate the crowning of the new Queen.

Saxe Street party

Names include Linda Smith, Mrs Roberts, Mrs Marshall, Mrs Rice, Pop Isaac, Mrs Norris, Mrs Woolway, Mrs Niblett, Mike Hinder, Bob Woolway, Mrs Bruford, Ian Northway, Diane Ellis, Sylvia Niblett, Ann Smale, Norris children and Francis Smith.

St James Church fancy dress parade for Sunday school children

Queen Elizabeth II visits Teignmouth
Her Majesty was driven along the Upper Den Carriageway, lined with school children.

Winners and Runners-Up at Teignmouth Tennis Tournament 1951
Players from across south Devon competed in the week-long, annual competition. Rows of seats were erected in stands overlooking the two courts nearest the bowling-green where the finals were staged. Joan Webber, Jean Boorer and Pauline Seaton stand together in the back row and Tony Graeme of Shaldon is forth from right. The Spirit of Teignmouth trimaran will be assembled on the site in 2006.

Pam Blackmore nee Catling

After securing a job as a junior clerk at Morgan Giles shipyard in 1946, Pam worked under the guidance of Jimmy Gardiner. She was deputed to telephone the Harbour Master and request him to open up the span of Shaldon Bridge to allow for a high-masted yacht to pass through. That request marked an unforgettable moment in her limited experience of life and work.

The bridge across the Teign to Shaldon, 1940s
The opening span shows up as a dark stripe behind the head of the toll collector. This practice ended when Devon County Council purchased the bridge and abolished tolls in 1949.

Chapter 6

Remember

*Features and corners changed or gone forever............reminders
of war.........an ever-changing town.*

B J Wareham's Shop
*Local professional photographer, B J Wareham, created many images of
Teignmouth during the post-war period at his premises in Bitton Street.*

Broadbear's Garage, 1940s
The premises occupied a site between Esplanade and Regent Street, in a little cutting recently signed as The Street With No Name.

Lighthouse and Ness
Teignmouth's coat of arms is picked out in tiny plants on the raised bed at the entrance to the Point car park. A woman and two little children walk along the prom' where a single string of fairy lights was installed in the late 1930s.

Jubilee Shelter, Eastcliff

A Fleet Air Arm plane, a Blackburn Skua was towing a target offshore when it ran into trouble either from friendly fire or engine failure. It came down in the sea about 50 yards offshore at Eastcliff. The pilot, who wore a luxuriant beard, was not hurt and enjoyed the notoriety, according to Jim Stowers. No immediate attempt was made to recover the craft and it was removed many years later after becoming a danger to swimmers. Part of the plane's undercarriage was still visible in 1946 according to Ken Bennett who recalls that the sand level was so low, it was possible to walk underneath the outfall pipe. In the war years, he often took Cheeky the dog to the seafront and if the ball rolled under the rolls of barbed wire, strewn along the promenade, Cheeky did not hesitate to retrieve it. The Den Pavilion's south side was painted or screened in white to make flags show up when troops signalled in semaphore across to Ness House.

Christchurch

A nissen hut served as a temporary place of worship and community centre for the people of west Teignmouth. The building that replaced it in the mid 1950s was sold for conversion to a dwelling in the 1990s.

Tom Radford

The National Fire Service took over County Garage after the town hall was bombed in August 1942. It was spacious and had a drill yard at the side. A large concrete water tank was installed so that appliances could take on water if a hydrant had been destroyed. Three or four engines were kept there until an architect said that the garage floor was not strong enough. A new station was created within a block of lock-up garages at the end of First Avenue in 1947/8. It was intended to be temporary but nearly 60 years passed before the building of the new station began on Higher Brook Street.

Fire appliance on Strand, outside Morgan Giles shipyard buildings, 1950s

Bomb crater near Headway Cross, 2005
The bramble-filled crater, close to Inverteign School is a forgotten relic from the 22nd and final air raid in the area that occurred in May 1944.

Seafront Mine
Positioned at a spot called The Gun, on the promenade, this mine is a stark reminder of those sought-out and blown up by our servicemen.

The Guinness Clock
Created for the Festival of Britain in 1951, this quirky artwork later appeared on the seafront, close to the pier.

Sunken Garden, 1930s
Archie Palmer installed the illuminations in this much-admired feature, stocked with night-scented plants. During the war, it had been surrounded with sandbags and used for a gun emplacement. It was removed in 1990 as part of extensive storm damage works.

Teignmouth Grammar School Memorial, 2005
The names of students who lost their lives are recorded on this plaque, in the entrance corridor of Teignmouth Community College.

Pilot Sergeant Gerald Edworthy

In December 2004, a number of relatives of Pilot Sergeant Gerald Edworthy, a pupil of Teignmouth Grammar School gathered to witness the unveiling of a commemorative plaque to his memory, presented by The Battle of Britain Historical Society. Gerald Edworthy, who had lived in Speranza Grove began pilot training in 1938 and flew solo after only six days. He served with 46 squadron, flying Hurricanes in Norway and took part in the Battle of Britain. He was killed in action in September 1940, at the age of 25 years.

Wings for Victory War Savings Campaign 1943

Salute the Soldier Week 1944

The pair of memorial tablets are displayed in the inner hall of Bitton House.

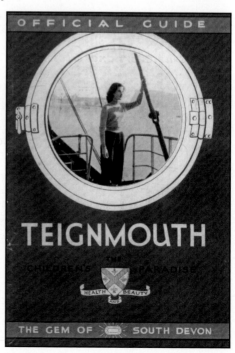

Teignmouth Guide book, late 1940s

When Teignmouth was re-building its reputation as a holiday resort in the post war years, Donald Sharpe who worked for the Urban District Council requested a 17-year old to write the Teignmouth Guide under her name R. Isabella Thomas. Ivy Hindley photographed Ruth on a cargo boat in Teignmouth harbour for the front cover.

Teignmouth Gas Works and Railway line 1950s

Opened in 1839, the works were damaged by canon fire and machine gun bullets during a raid on 13 August 1942. The two large cylindrical holders were perforated and Mr Higham the Manager, who lived overlooking the works, ran to turn off the gas supply and get the holes plugged with clay to retain the supply. The old buildings have declined but boat builder, Chris Humphrey has occupied the site in recent years.

Nellie (Nurse) Bell

Nellie's husband, a world war one veteran died young from pneumonia. She brought up their three children and ran a greengrocery shop in Regent Street. Her son joined the RAF in 1939 and was shot down over France. Nellie joined the Red Cross, did fire watching from the roof of the Riviera and helped air raid wardens. Her home, Esplanade House, survived the bomb that destroyed the large hotel next door. She volunteered to provide the Last Offices to air raid victims and laid them out with dignity in the mortuary at Gales Hill. After the war she joined the British Legion and organized tea dances in the pier ballroom. Nellie was an unsung heroine.

The former mortuary at Gales Hill, currently a fishermen's store

A new "village" in west Teignmouth
More than 100 prefabricated houses were built on Kingsway in the late 1940s, on a prominent position above Broadmeadow.

P5002 in the harbour
A post-war MTB built at Morgan Giles shipyard in 1951. The Sanders & Roe design had wood planking and aluminium was used for the frame and bulkheads. Kingsway Estate is visible beyond its bows.

Gay Charger P1047, 1953

Gay Charger was the 100th naval vessel built in the yard. She and her sister ship, Gay Charioteer were 71ft, Vosper designed MTBs. They had the honour of escorting the Royal Yacht Britannia on the river Thames when HM The Queen returned from her first royal tour in 1954.

Teign View Place, c. 1960

Many years would pass before the occupants of the cottages opening onto the back beach would enhance their homes with patios and sliding doors. The shipyard buildings fell into a slow decline and the Morgan Giles business ended in 1968.

Fraser's Store, Waterloo Street

The shop with a massive stock of garments and haberdashery, stretched through to Wellington Street. It changed ownership to Hitchens and traded for many more years until 2001.

Cockings' Dairy
Standing next to the Gospel Hall, the shop was one of many that suffered trade-loss after closure of the east section of Bitton Street.

Teignmouth Railway Station, 1949
Six boxes containing 150 live chicks, hatched by Underhill & Oaksford of Shaldon, went by rail to London and arrived by air in Belgium next day. Mr Tremethick, Station Master oversees the departure with Mr Underhill, second right.

Bill Ballinger

A renowned chef at the Royal Hotel in the 1960s, Bill was well known to local people. He was rescued after a torpedo hit his tank landing craft in the north sea and received injuries to his eye and ear that troubled him for the remainder of his life. Bill cooked for troops at the jungle battlefront and took part in the Burma Campaign. He was mentioned in despatches for his involvement in the Rhine crossings. He is pictured on parade at Remembrance Sunday, 1998 - the last he was able to attend. Bill died at dawn on 15 August 1999, the 54th anniversary of Victory in Japan

Memorial stone, Botanical Gardens, Shaldon
The inscription reads " In Commemoration of the Nurses for their devoted and professional care during the 1941-1945 Burma Campaign. Burma Star Association. April 1997.

Memorial stone, Torrington

David Lawrey, aged 8 of Teignmouth perished with four other children in a fire at Sydney House in 1942. The memorial stone was erected in 2004.

The Den, early 1950s

The bandstand was the centre of focus for numerous carnivals, presentations and commemorations. Teignmouth and it's people had to turn and face a new world with an ever-quickening pace and never-ending cycle of change.

LEST WE FORGET

Teignmouth commemorated the 60th Anniversary of Victory in Europe and Japan on 19th June 2005. In his address, EJE Stowers QPM included the following pieces in homage to the armed forces and civilians.

Merchant Navy and Royal Navy

There are no roses on a sailor's grave
No lilies on an ocean wave
We, the old watch, whose lives were saved
We pray the young will salute the brave

Royal Air Force

Do not despair for Johnny Head-in-the-Air
He sleeps as sound as Johnny-Underground
Fetch out no shroud for Johnny-in-the-Cloud
And keep your tears for him in after years
Better by far for Johnny-the-Bright-Star
To keep your head and see his children fed

Army and all Auxiliaries including civilians

O valiant heart, who to your glory came
Through dust of conflict and through battle flame
Tranquil you lie, your knightly virtue proved
Your memory hallowed in the land you loved

On a stone memorial on a jungle hill in Burma is the inscription

When you go home
Tell them of us and say
For your tomorrow- we gave our today